C-1958   CAREER EXAMINATION SERIES

This is your
PASSBOOK for...

Head Custodian

Test Preparation Study Guide
Questions & Answers

NATIONAL LEARNING CORPORATION®

COPYRIGHT NOTICE

This book is SOLELY intended for, is sold ONLY to, and its use is RESTRICTED to individual, bona fide applicants or candidates who qualify by virtue of having seriously filed applications for appropriate license, certificate, professional and/or promotional advancement, higher school matriculation, scholarship, or other legitimate requirements of education and/or governmental authorities.

This book is NOT intended for use, class instruction, tutoring, training, duplication, copying, reprinting, excerption, or adaptation, etc., by:

1) Other publishers
2) Proprietors and/or Instructors of "Coaching" and/or Preparatory Courses
3) Personnel and/or Training Divisions of commercial, industrial, and governmental organizations
4) Schools, colleges, or universities and/or their departments and staffs, including teachers and other personnel
5) Testing Agencies or Bureaus
6) Study groups which seek by the purchase of a single volume to copy and/or duplicate and/or adapt this material for use by the group as a whole without having purchased individual volumes for each of the members of the group
7) Et al.

Such persons would be in violation of appropriate Federal and State statutes.

PROVISION OF LICENSING AGREEMENTS – Recognized educational, commercial, industrial, and governmental institutions and organizations, and others legitimately engaged in educational pursuits, including training, testing, and measurement activities, may address request for a licensing agreement to the copyright owners, who will determine whether, and under what conditions, including fees and charges, the materials in this book may be used them. In other words, a licensing facility exists for the legitimate use of the material in this book on other than an individual basis. However, it is asseverated and affirmed here that the material in this book CANNOT be used without the receipt of the express permission of such a licensing agreement from the Publishers. Inquiries re licensing should be addressed to the company, attention rights and permissions department.

All rights reserved, including the right of reproduction in whole or in part, in any form or by any means, electronic or mechanical, including photocopying, recording, or by any information storage and retrieval system, without permission in writing from the Publisher.

Copyright © 2024 by
National Learning Corporation

212 Michael Drive, Syosset, NY 11791
(516) 921-8888 • www.passbooks.com
E-mail: info@passbooks.com

PUBLISHED IN THE UNITED STATES OF AMERICA

PASSBOOK® SERIES

THE *PASSBOOK® SERIES* has been created to prepare applicants and candidates for the ultimate academic battlefield – the examination room.

At some time in our lives, each and every one of us may be required to take an examination – for validation, matriculation, admission, qualification, registration, certification, or licensure.

Based on the assumption that every applicant or candidate has met the basic formal educational standards, has taken the required number of courses, and read the necessary texts, the *PASSBOOK® SERIES* furnishes the one special preparation which may assure passing with confidence, instead of failing with insecurity. Examination questions – together with answers – are furnished as the basic vehicle for study so that the mysteries of the examination and its compounding difficulties may be eliminated or diminished by a sure method.

This book is meant to help you pass your examination provided that you qualify and are serious in your objective.

The entire field is reviewed through the huge store of content information which is succinctly presented through a provocative and challenging approach – the question-and-answer method.

A climate of success is established by furnishing the correct answers at the end of each test.

You soon learn to recognize types of questions, forms of questions, and patterns of questioning. You may even begin to anticipate expected outcomes.

You perceive that many questions are repeated or adapted so that you can gain acute insights, which may enable you to score many sure points.

You learn how to confront new questions, or types of questions, and to attack them confidently and work out the correct answers.

You note objectives and emphases, and recognize pitfalls and dangers, so that you may make positive educational adjustments.

Moreover, you are kept fully informed in relation to new concepts, methods, practices, and directions in the field.

You discover that you are actually taking the examination all the time: you are preparing for the examination by "taking" an examination, not by reading extraneous and/or supererogatory textbooks.

In short, this PASSBOOK®, used directedly, should be an important factor in helping you to pass your test.

HEAD CUSTODIAN

DUTIES:
Under general supervision, employees in this class are responsible for the efficient and economical maintenance of a library or school facility, and have complete charge of building cleaning, maintenance and minor repair activities. In large districts, this class is usually in charge of only one building under the general supervision of a higher level administrator. In smaller districts, a Head Custodian may have charge over two or more buildings and be responsible to the Chief Custodian, Business Manager, Assistant Superintendent or an equivalent administrator. Considerable independent judgment is usually involved in carrying out the responsibilities of this position. Supervision is exercised over subordinate custodians and/or maintenance personnel.

EXAMPLES OF TYPICAL TASKS:
An employee in this class is responsible for scheduling and supervising the work of a number of custodial workers engaged in a variety of cleaning tasks. Duties require the exercise of independent judgment in planning work methods, scheduling work assignments and reviewing the work performed. Operates and performs minor maintenance work on electrical, plumbing, heating and ventilation systems including low and high pressure steam boilers and oil burners. May supervise minor ground maintenance work including snow removal, grass cutting and the raking of leaves. Maintains necessary records and prepares required reports relating to personnel, supplies, equipment and work performed. Does related work as required.

SCOPE OF THE EAMINATION
1. The written test will be designed to test for knowledge, skills, and/or abilities in such areas as:
2. **Ability to read and follow written instructions** - These questions test for the ability to read, understand and apply written instructions for performing tasks similar to those encountered on the job. All the information needed to answer these questions will be provided in the test booklet.
3. **Building cleaning** - These questions test for knowledge of basic principles and practices of building cleaning. They cover such areas as equipment, tools, supplies, methods and procedures for cleaning different types of surfaces and materials under various, commonly occurring circumstances.
4. **Building operation and maintenance** - These questions test for knowledge of the basic principles, practices and techniques essential to the correct operation and maintenance of public buildings. They cover such areas as building maintenance; preventive maintenance, and minor repair of electrical and plumbing systems; methods and equipment for snow removal; building safety and equipment storage.
5. **Operation and routine maintenance of heating, ventilating and air conditioning systems** - These questions test for knowledge of basic principles, practices and techniques essential to the correct operation and maintenance of heating, ventilating and air conditioning systems, including such areas as minor cleaning; room temperature and building ventilation control; steam, hot water and hot air heating systems; boiler operation; troubleshooting air conditioning system problems, and proper maintenance of air conditioning systems.
6. **Supervision and training** - These questions test for the knowledge required by a supervisor to set goals, plan and organize work, train workers in how to do their jobs, and direct workers towards meeting established goals. The supervisory questions cover such areas as assigning and reviewing work, evaluating performance, maintaining work quality, motivating employees, increasing efficiency, and dealing with problems that may arise on the job. The training questions cover such areas as determining the necessity for training, selecting appropriate training methods, and evaluating the effectiveness of training.

HOW TO TAKE A TEST

I. YOU MUST PASS AN EXAMINATION

A. WHAT EVERY CANDIDATE SHOULD KNOW
Examination applicants often ask us for help in preparing for the written test. What can I study in advance? What kinds of questions will be asked? How will the test be given? How will the papers be graded?

As an applicant for a civil service examination, you may be wondering about some of these things. Our purpose here is to suggest effective methods of advance study and to describe civil service examinations.

Your chances for success on this examination can be increased if you know how to prepare. Those "pre-examination jitters" can be reduced if you know what to expect. You can even experience an adventure in good citizenship if you know why civil service exams are given.

B. WHY ARE CIVIL SERVICE EXAMINATIONS GIVEN?
Civil service examinations are important to you in two ways. As a citizen, you want public jobs filled by employees who know how to do their work. As a job seeker, you want a fair chance to compete for that job on an equal footing with other candidates. The best-known means of accomplishing this two-fold goal is the competitive examination.

Exams are widely publicized throughout the nation. They may be administered for jobs in federal, state, city, municipal, town or village governments or agencies.

Any citizen may apply, with some limitations, such as the age or residence of applicants. Your experience and education may be reviewed to see whether you meet the requirements for the particular examination. When these requirements exist, they are reasonable and applied consistently to all applicants. Thus, a competitive examination may cause you some uneasiness now, but it is your privilege and safeguard.

C. HOW ARE CIVIL SERVICE EXAMS DEVELOPED?
Examinations are carefully written by trained technicians who are specialists in the field known as "psychological measurement," in consultation with recognized authorities in the field of work that the test will cover. These experts recommend the subject matter areas or skills to be tested; only those knowledges or skills important to your success on the job are included. The most reliable books and source materials available are used as references. Together, the experts and technicians judge the difficulty level of the questions.

Test technicians know how to phrase questions so that the problem is clearly stated. Their ethics do not permit "trick" or "catch" questions. Questions may have been tried out on sample groups, or subjected to statistical analysis, to determine their usefulness.

Written tests are often used in combination with performance tests, ratings of training and experience, and oral interviews. All of these measures combine to form the best-known means of finding the right person for the right job.

II. HOW TO PASS THE WRITTEN TEST

A. NATURE OF THE EXAMINATION

To prepare intelligently for civil service examinations, you should know how they differ from school examinations you have taken. In school you were assigned certain definite pages to read or subjects to cover. The examination questions were quite detailed and usually emphasized memory. Civil service exams, on the other hand, try to discover your present ability to perform the duties of a position, plus your potentiality to learn these duties. In other words, a civil service exam attempts to predict how successful you will be. Questions cover such a broad area that they cannot be as minute and detailed as school exam questions.

In the public service similar kinds of work, or positions, are grouped together in one "class." This process is known as *position-classification*. All the positions in a class are paid according to the salary range for that class. One class title covers all of these positions, and they are all tested by the same examination.

B. FOUR BASIC STEPS

1) Study the announcement

How, then, can you know what subjects to study? Our best answer is: "Learn as much as possible about the class of positions for which you've applied." The exam will test the knowledge, skills and abilities needed to do the work.

Your most valuable source of information about the position you want is the official exam announcement. This announcement lists the training and experience qualifications. Check these standards and apply only if you come reasonably close to meeting them.

The brief description of the position in the examination announcement offers some clues to the subjects which will be tested. Think about the job itself. Review the duties in your mind. Can you perform them, or are there some in which you are rusty? Fill in the blank spots in your preparation.

Many jurisdictions preview the written test in the exam announcement by including a section called "Knowledge and Abilities Required," "Scope of the Examination," or some similar heading. Here you will find out specifically what fields will be tested.

2) Review your own background

Once you learn in general what the position is all about, and what you need to know to do the work, ask yourself which subjects you already know fairly well and which need improvement. You may wonder whether to concentrate on improving your strong areas or on building some background in your fields of weakness. When the announcement has specified "some knowledge" or "considerable knowledge," or has used adjectives like "beginning principles of…" or "advanced … methods," you can get a clue as to the number and difficulty of questions to be asked in any given field. More questions, and hence broader coverage, would be included for those subjects which are more important in the work. Now weigh your strengths and weaknesses against the job requirements and prepare accordingly.

3) Determine the level of the position

Another way to tell how intensively you should prepare is to understand the level of the job for which you are applying. Is it the entering level? In other words, is this the position in which beginners in a field of work are hired? Or is it an intermediate or advanced level? Sometimes this is indicated by such words as "Junior" or "Senior" in the class title. Other jurisdictions use Roman numerals to designate the level – Clerk I, Clerk II, for example. The word "Supervisor" sometimes appears in the title. If the level is not indicated by the title, check the description of duties. Will you be working under very close supervision, or will you have responsibility for independent decisions in this work?

4) Choose appropriate study materials

Now that you know the subjects to be examined and the relative amount of each subject to be covered, you can choose suitable study materials. For beginning level jobs, or even advanced ones, if you have a pronounced weakness in some aspect of your training, read a modern, standard textbook in that field. Be sure it is up to date and has general coverage. Such books are normally available at your library, and the librarian will be glad to help you locate one. For entry-level positions, questions of appropriate difficulty are chosen – neither highly advanced questions, nor those too simple. Such questions require careful thought but not advanced training.

If the position for which you are applying is technical or advanced, you will read more advanced, specialized material. If you are already familiar with the basic principles of your field, elementary textbooks would waste your time. Concentrate on advanced textbooks and technical periodicals. Think through the concepts and review difficult problems in your field.

These are all general sources. You can get more ideas on your own initiative, following these leads. For example, training manuals and publications of the government agency which employs workers in your field can be useful, particularly for technical and professional positions. A letter or visit to the government department involved may result in more specific study suggestions, and certainly will provide you with a more definite idea of the exact nature of the position you are seeking.

III. KINDS OF TESTS

Tests are used for purposes other than measuring knowledge and ability to perform specified duties. For some positions, it is equally important to test ability to make adjustments to new situations or to profit from training. In others, basic mental abilities not dependent on information are essential. Questions which test these things may not appear as pertinent to the duties of the position as those which test for knowledge and information. Yet they are often highly important parts of a fair examination. For very general questions, it is almost impossible to help you direct your study efforts. What we can do is to point out some of the more common of these general abilities needed in public service positions and describe some typical questions.

1) General information

Broad, general information has been found useful for predicting job success in some kinds of work. This is tested in a variety of ways, from vocabulary lists to questions about current events. Basic background in some field of work, such as sociology or economics, may be sampled in a group of questions. Often these are principles which have become familiar to most persons through exposure rather than through formal training. It is difficult to advise you how to study for these questions; being alert to the world around you is our best suggestion.

2) Verbal ability

An example of an ability needed in many positions is verbal or language ability. Verbal ability is, in brief, the ability to use and understand words. Vocabulary and grammar tests are typical measures of this ability. Reading comprehension or paragraph interpretation questions are common in many kinds of civil service tests. You are given a paragraph of written material and asked to find its central meaning.

3) Numerical ability

Number skills can be tested by the familiar arithmetic problem, by checking paired lists of numbers to see which are alike and which are different, or by interpreting charts and graphs. In the latter test, a graph may be printed in the test booklet which you are asked to use as the basis for answering questions.

4) Observation

A popular test for law-enforcement positions is the observation test. A picture is shown to you for several minutes, then taken away. Questions about the picture test your ability to observe both details and larger elements.

5) Following directions

In many positions in the public service, the employee must be able to carry out written instructions dependably and accurately. You may be given a chart with several columns, each column listing a variety of information. The questions require you to carry out directions involving the information given in the chart.

6) Skills and aptitudes

Performance tests effectively measure some manual skills and aptitudes. When the skill is one in which you are trained, such as typing or shorthand, you can practice. These tests are often very much like those given in business school or high school courses. For many of the other skills and aptitudes, however, no short-time preparation can be made. Skills and abilities natural to you or that you have developed throughout your lifetime are being tested.

Many of the general questions just described provide all the data needed to answer the questions and ask you to use your reasoning ability to find the answers. Your best preparation for these tests, as well as for tests of facts and ideas, is to be at your physical and mental best. You, no doubt, have your own methods of getting into an exam-taking mood and keeping "in shape." The next section lists some ideas on this subject.

IV. KINDS OF QUESTIONS

Only rarely is the "essay" question, which you answer in narrative form, used in civil service tests. Civil service tests are usually of the short-answer type. Full instructions for answering these questions will be given to you at the examination. But in case this is your first experience with short-answer questions and separate answer sheets, here is what you need to know:

1) Multiple-choice Questions

Most popular of the short-answer questions is the "multiple choice" or "best answer" question. It can be used, for example, to test for factual knowledge, ability to solve problems or judgment in meeting situations found at work.

A multiple-choice question is normally one of three types—
- It can begin with an incomplete statement followed by several possible endings. You are to find the one ending which *best* completes the statement, although some of the others may not be entirely wrong.
- It can also be a complete statement in the form of a question which is answered by choosing one of the statements listed.

- It can be in the form of a problem – again you select the best answer.

Here is an example of a multiple-choice question with a discussion which should give you some clues as to the method for choosing the right answer:

When an employee has a complaint about his assignment, the action which will *best* help him overcome his difficulty is to
- A. discuss his difficulty with his coworkers
- B. take the problem to the head of the organization
- C. take the problem to the person who gave him the assignment
- D. say nothing to anyone about his complaint

In answering this question, you should study each of the choices to find which is best. Consider choice "A" – Certainly an employee may discuss his complaint with fellow employees, but no change or improvement can result, and the complaint remains unresolved. Choice "B" is a poor choice since the head of the organization probably does not know what assignment you have been given, and taking your problem to him is known as "going over the head" of the supervisor. The supervisor, or person who made the assignment, is the person who can clarify it or correct any injustice. Choice "C" is, therefore, correct. To say nothing, as in choice "D," is unwise. Supervisors have and interest in knowing the problems employees are facing, and the employee is seeking a solution to his problem.

2) True/False Questions

The "true/false" or "right/wrong" form of question is sometimes used. Here a complete statement is given. Your job is to decide whether the statement is right or wrong.

SAMPLE: A roaming cell-phone call to a nearby city costs less than a non-roaming call to a distant city.

This statement is wrong, or false, since roaming calls are more expensive.

This is not a complete list of all possible question forms, although most of the others are variations of these common types. You will always get complete directions for answering questions. Be sure you understand *how* to mark your answers – ask questions until you do.

V. RECORDING YOUR ANSWERS

Computer terminals are used more and more today for many different kinds of exams.

For an examination with very few applicants, you may be told to record your answers in the test booklet itself. Separate answer sheets are much more common. If this separate answer sheet is to be scored by machine – and this is often the case – it is highly important that you mark your answers correctly in order to get credit.

An electronic scoring machine is often used in civil service offices because of the speed with which papers can be scored. Machine-scored answer sheets must be marked with a pencil, which will be given to you. This pencil has a high graphite content which responds to the electronic scoring machine. As a matter of fact, stray dots may register as answers, so do not let your pencil rest on the answer sheet while you are pondering the correct answer. Also, if your pencil lead breaks or is otherwise defective, ask for another.

Since the answer sheet will be dropped in a slot in the scoring machine, be careful not to bend the corners or get the paper crumpled.

The answer sheet normally has five vertical columns of numbers, with 30 numbers to a column. These numbers correspond to the question numbers in your test booklet. After each number, going across the page are four or five pairs of dotted lines. These short dotted lines have small letters or numbers above them. The first two pairs may also have a "T" or "F" above the letters. This indicates that the first two pairs only are to be used if the questions are of the true-false type. If the questions are multiple choice, disregard the "T" and "F" and pay attention only to the small letters or numbers.

Answer your questions in the manner of the sample that follows:

32. The largest city in the United States is
    A. Washington, D.C.
    B. New York City
    C. Chicago
    D. Detroit
    E. San Francisco

1) Choose the answer you think is best. (New York City is the largest, so "B" is correct.)
2) Find the row of dotted lines numbered the same as the question you are answering. (Find row number 32)
3) Find the pair of dotted lines corresponding to the answer. (Find the pair of lines under the mark "B.")
4) Make a solid black mark between the dotted lines.

VI. BEFORE THE TEST

Common sense will help you find procedures to follow to get ready for an examination. Too many of us, however, overlook these sensible measures. Indeed, nervousness and fatigue have been found to be the most serious reasons why applicants fail to do their best on civil service tests. Here is a list of reminders:

- Begin your preparation early – Don't wait until the last minute to go scurrying around for books and materials or to find out what the position is all about.
- Prepare continuously – An hour a night for a week is better than an all-night cram session. This has been definitely established. What is more, a night a week for a month will return better dividends than crowding your study into a shorter period of time.
- Locate the place of the exam – You have been sent a notice telling you when and where to report for the examination. If the location is in a different town or otherwise unfamiliar to you, it would be well to inquire the best route and learn something about the building.
- Relax the night before the test – Allow your mind to rest. Do not study at all that night. Plan some mild recreation or diversion; then go to bed early and get a good night's sleep.
- Get up early enough to make a leisurely trip to the place for the test – This way unforeseen events, traffic snarls, unfamiliar buildings, etc. will not upset you.
- Dress comfortably – A written test is not a fashion show. You will be known by number and not by name, so wear something comfortable.

- Leave excess paraphernalia at home – Shopping bags and odd bundles will get in your way. You need bring only the items mentioned in the official notice you received; usually everything you need is provided. Do not bring reference books to the exam. They will only confuse those last minutes and be taken away from you when in the test room.
- Arrive somewhat ahead of time – If because of transportation schedules you must get there very early, bring a newspaper or magazine to take your mind off yourself while waiting.
- Locate the examination room – When you have found the proper room, you will be directed to the seat or part of the room where you will sit. Sometimes you are given a sheet of instructions to read while you are waiting. Do not fill out any forms until you are told to do so; just read them and be prepared.
- Relax and prepare to listen to the instructions
- If you have any physical problem that may keep you from doing your best, be sure to tell the test administrator. If you are sick or in poor health, you really cannot do your best on the exam. You can come back and take the test some other time.

VII. AT THE TEST

The day of the test is here and you have the test booklet in your hand. The temptation to get going is very strong. Caution! There is more to success than knowing the right answers. You must know how to identify your papers and understand variations in the type of short-answer question used in this particular examination. Follow these suggestions for maximum results from your efforts:

1) Cooperate with the monitor

The test administrator has a duty to create a situation in which you can be as much at ease as possible. He will give instructions, tell you when to begin, check to see that you are marking your answer sheet correctly, and so on. He is not there to guard you, although he will see that your competitors do not take unfair advantage. He wants to help you do your best.

2) Listen to all instructions

Don't jump the gun! Wait until you understand all directions. In most civil service tests you get more time than you need to answer the questions. So don't be in a hurry. Read each word of instructions until you clearly understand the meaning. Study the examples, listen to all announcements and follow directions. Ask questions if you do not understand what to do.

3) Identify your papers

Civil service exams are usually identified by number only. You will be assigned a number; you must not put your name on your test papers. Be sure to copy your number correctly. Since more than one exam may be given, copy your exact examination title.

4) Plan your time

Unless you are told that a test is a "speed" or "rate of work" test, speed itself is usually not important. Time enough to answer all the questions will be provided, but this does not mean that you have all day. An overall time limit has been set. Divide the total time (in minutes) by the number of questions to determine the approximate time you have for each question.

5) Do not linger over difficult questions

If you come across a difficult question, mark it with a paper clip (useful to have along) and come back to it when you have been through the booklet. One caution if you do this – be sure to skip a number on your answer sheet as well. Check often to be sure that you have not lost your place and that you are marking in the row numbered the same as the question you are answering.

6) Read the questions

Be sure you know what the question asks! Many capable people are unsuccessful because they failed to *read* the questions correctly.

7) Answer all questions

Unless you have been instructed that a penalty will be deducted for incorrect answers, it is better to guess than to omit a question.

8) Speed tests

It is often better NOT to guess on speed tests. It has been found that on timed tests people are tempted to spend the last few seconds before time is called in marking answers at random – without even reading them – in the hope of picking up a few extra points. To discourage this practice, the instructions may warn you that your score will be "corrected" for guessing. That is, a penalty will be applied. The incorrect answers will be deducted from the correct ones, or some other penalty formula will be used.

9) Review your answers

If you finish before time is called, go back to the questions you guessed or omitted to give them further thought. Review other answers if you have time.

10) Return your test materials

If you are ready to leave before others have finished or time is called, take ALL your materials to the monitor and leave quietly. Never take any test material with you. The monitor can discover whose papers are not complete, and taking a test booklet may be grounds for disqualification.

VIII. EXAMINATION TECHNIQUES

1) Read the general instructions carefully. These are usually printed on the first page of the exam booklet. As a rule, these instructions refer to the timing of the examination; the fact that you should not start work until the signal and must stop work at a signal, etc. If there are any *special* instructions, such as a choice of questions to be answered, make sure that you note this instruction carefully.

2) When you are ready to start work on the examination, that is as soon as the signal has been given, read the instructions to each question booklet, underline any key words or phrases, such as *least, best, outline, describe* and the like. In this way you will tend to answer as requested rather than discover on reviewing your paper that you *listed without describing*, that you selected the *worst* choice rather than the *best* choice, etc.

3) If the examination is of the objective or multiple-choice type – that is, each question will also give a series of possible answers: A, B, C or D, and you are called upon to select the best answer and write the letter next to that answer on your answer paper – it is advisable to start answering each question in turn. There may be anywhere from 50 to 100 such questions in the three or four hours allotted and you can see how much time would be taken if you read through all the questions before beginning to answer any. Furthermore, if you come across a question or group of questions which you know would be difficult to answer, it would undoubtedly affect your handling of all the other questions.

4) If the examination is of the essay type and contains but a few questions, it is a moot point as to whether you should read all the questions before starting to answer any one. Of course, if you are given a choice – say five out of seven and the like – then it is essential to read all the questions so you can eliminate the two that are most difficult. If, however, you are asked to answer all the questions, there may be danger in trying to answer the easiest one first because you may find that you will spend too much time on it. The best technique is to answer the first question, then proceed to the second, etc.

5) Time your answers. Before the exam begins, write down the time it started, then add the time allowed for the examination and write down the time it must be completed, then divide the time available somewhat as follows:
    - If 3-1/2 hours are allowed, that would be 210 minutes. If you have 80 objective-type questions, that would be an average of 2-1/2 minutes per question. Allow yourself no more than 2 minutes per question, or a total of 160 minutes, which will permit about 50 minutes to review.
    - If for the time allotment of 210 minutes there are 7 essay questions to answer, that would average about 30 minutes a question. Give yourself only 25 minutes per question so that you have about 35 minutes to review.

6) The most important instruction is to *read each question* and make sure you know what is wanted. The second most important instruction is to *time yourself properly* so that you answer every question. The third most important instruction is to *answer every question*. Guess if you have to but include something for each question. Remember that you will receive no credit for a blank and will probably receive some credit if you write something in answer to an essay question. If you guess a letter – say "B" for a multiple-choice question – you may have guessed right. If you leave a blank as an answer to a multiple-choice question, the examiners may respect your feelings but it will not add a point to your score. Some exams may penalize you for wrong answers, so in such cases *only*, you may not want to guess unless you have some basis for your answer.

7) Suggestions
    a. Objective-type questions
        1. Examine the question booklet for proper sequence of pages and questions
        2. Read all instructions carefully
        3. Skip any question which seems too difficult; return to it after all other questions have been answered
        4. Apportion your time properly; do not spend too much time on any single question or group of questions

5. Note and underline key words – *all, most, fewest, least, best, worst, same, opposite*, etc.
6. Pay particular attention to negatives
7. Note unusual option, e.g., unduly long, short, complex, different or similar in content to the body of the question
8. Observe the use of "hedging" words – *probably, may, most likely*, etc.
9. Make sure that your answer is put next to the same number as the question
10. Do not second-guess unless you have good reason to believe the second answer is definitely more correct
11. Cross out original answer if you decide another answer is more accurate; do not erase until you are ready to hand your paper in
12. Answer all questions; guess unless instructed otherwise
13. Leave time for review

b. Essay questions
1. Read each question carefully
2. Determine exactly what is wanted. Underline key words or phrases.
3. Decide on outline or paragraph answer
4. Include many different points and elements unless asked to develop any one or two points or elements
5. Show impartiality by giving pros and cons unless directed to select one side only
6. Make and write down any assumptions you find necessary to answer the questions
7. Watch your English, grammar, punctuation and choice of words
8. Time your answers; don't crowd material

8) Answering the essay question

Most essay questions can be answered by framing the specific response around several key words or ideas. Here are a few such key words or ideas:

M's: manpower, materials, methods, money, management
P's: purpose, program, policy, plan, procedure, practice, problems, pitfalls, personnel, public relations

a. Six basic steps in handling problems:
1. Preliminary plan and background development
2. Collect information, data and facts
3. Analyze and interpret information, data and facts
4. Analyze and develop solutions as well as make recommendations
5. Prepare report and sell recommendations
6. Install recommendations and follow up effectiveness

b. Pitfalls to avoid
1. *Taking things for granted* – A statement of the situation does not necessarily imply that each of the elements is necessarily true; for example, a complaint may be invalid and biased so that all that can be taken for granted is that a complaint has been registered

2. *Considering only one side of a situation* – Wherever possible, indicate several alternatives and then point out the reasons you selected the best one
3. *Failing to indicate follow up* – Whenever your answer indicates action on your part, make certain that you will take proper follow-up action to see how successful your recommendations, procedures or actions turn out to be
4. *Taking too long in answering any single question* – Remember to time your answers properly

IX. AFTER THE TEST

Scoring procedures differ in detail among civil service jurisdictions although the general principles are the same. Whether the papers are hand-scored or graded by machine we have described, they are nearly always graded by number. That is, the person who marks the paper knows only the number – never the name – of the applicant. Not until all the papers have been graded will they be matched with names. If other tests, such as training and experience or oral interview ratings have been given, scores will be combined. Different parts of the examination usually have different weights. For example, the written test might count 60 percent of the final grade, and a rating of training and experience 40 percent. In many jurisdictions, veterans will have a certain number of points added to their grades.

After the final grade has been determined, the names are placed in grade order and an eligible list is established. There are various methods for resolving ties between those who get the same final grade – probably the most common is to place first the name of the person whose application was received first. Job offers are made from the eligible list in the order the names appear on it. You will be notified of your grade and your rank as soon as all these computations have been made. This will be done as rapidly as possible.

People who are found to meet the requirements in the announcement are called "eligibles." Their names are put on a list of eligible candidates. An eligible's chances of getting a job depend on how high he stands on this list and how fast agencies are filling jobs from the list.

When a job is to be filled from a list of eligibles, the agency asks for the names of people on the list of eligibles for that job. When the civil service commission receives this request, it sends to the agency the names of the three people highest on this list. Or, if the job to be filled has specialized requirements, the office sends the agency the names of the top three persons who meet these requirements from the general list.

The appointing officer makes a choice from among the three people whose names were sent to him. If the selected person accepts the appointment, the names of the others are put back on the list to be considered for future openings.

That is the rule in hiring from all kinds of eligible lists, whether they are for typist, carpenter, chemist, or something else. For every vacancy, the appointing officer has his choice of any one of the top three eligibles on the list. This explains why the person whose name is on top of the list sometimes does not get an appointment when some of the persons lower on the list do. If the appointing officer chooses the second or third eligible, the No. 1 eligible does not get a job at once, but stays on the list until he is appointed or the list is terminated.

X. HOW TO PASS THE INTERVIEW TEST

The examination for which you applied requires an oral interview test. You have already taken the written test and you are now being called for the interview test – the final part of the formal examination.

You may think that it is not possible to prepare for an interview test and that there are no procedures to follow during an interview. Our purpose is to point out some things you can do in advance that will help you and some good rules to follow and pitfalls to avoid while you are being interviewed.

What is an interview supposed to test?

The written examination is designed to test the technical knowledge and competence of the candidate; the oral is designed to evaluate intangible qualities, not readily measured otherwise, and to establish a list showing the relative fitness of each candidate – as measured against his competitors – for the position sought. Scoring is not on the basis of "right" and "wrong," but on a sliding scale of values ranging from "not passable" to "outstanding." As a matter of fact, it is possible to achieve a relatively low score without a single "incorrect" answer because of evident weakness in the qualities being measured.

Occasionally, an examination may consist entirely of an oral test – either an individual or a group oral. In such cases, information is sought concerning the technical knowledges and abilities of the candidate, since there has been no written examination for this purpose. More commonly, however, an oral test is used to supplement a written examination.

Who conducts interviews?

The composition of oral boards varies among different jurisdictions. In nearly all, a representative of the personnel department serves as chairman. One of the members of the board may be a representative of the department in which the candidate would work. In some cases, "outside experts" are used, and, frequently, a businessman or some other representative of the general public is asked to serve. Labor and management or other special groups may be represented. The aim is to secure the services of experts in the appropriate field.

However the board is composed, it is a good idea (and not at all improper or unethical) to ascertain in advance of the interview who the members are and what groups they represent. When you are introduced to them, you will have some idea of their backgrounds and interests, and at least you will not stutter and stammer over their names.

What should be done before the interview?

While knowledge about the board members is useful and takes some of the surprise element out of the interview, there is other preparation which is more substantive. It *is* possible to prepare for an oral interview – in several ways:

1) Keep a copy of your application and review it carefully before the interview

This may be the only document before the oral board, and the starting point of the interview. Know what education and experience you have listed there, and the sequence and dates of all of it. Sometimes the board will ask you to review the highlights of your experience for them; you should not have to hem and haw doing it.

2) Study the class specification and the examination announcement

Usually, the oral board has one or both of these to guide them. The qualities, characteristics or knowledges required by the position sought are stated in these documents. They offer valuable clues as to the nature of the oral interview. For example, if the job involves supervisory responsibilities, the announcement will usually indicate that knowledge of modern supervisory methods and the qualifications of the candidate as a supervisor will be tested. If so, you can expect such questions, frequently in the form of a hypothetical situation which you are expected to solve. NEVER go into an oral without knowledge of the duties and responsibilities of the job you seek.

3) Think through each qualification required

Try to visualize the kind of questions you would ask if you were a board member. How well could you answer them? Try especially to appraise your own knowledge and background in each area, *measured against the job sought*, and identify any areas in which you are weak. Be critical and realistic – do not flatter yourself.

4) Do some general reading in areas in which you feel you may be weak

For example, if the job involves supervision and your past experience has NOT, some general reading in supervisory methods and practices, particularly in the field of human relations, might be useful. Do NOT study agency procedures or detailed manuals. The oral board will be testing your understanding and capacity, not your memory.

5) Get a good night's sleep and watch your general health and mental attitude

You will want a clear head at the interview. Take care of a cold or any other minor ailment, and of course, no hangovers.

What should be done on the day of the interview?

Now comes the day of the interview itself. Give yourself plenty of time to get there. Plan to arrive somewhat ahead of the scheduled time, particularly if your appointment is in the fore part of the day. If a previous candidate fails to appear, the board might be ready for you a bit early. By early afternoon an oral board is almost invariably behind schedule if there are many candidates, and you may have to wait. Take along a book or magazine to read, or your application to review, but leave any extraneous material in the waiting room when you go in for your interview. In any event, relax and compose yourself.

The matter of dress is important. The board is forming impressions about you – from your experience, your manners, your attitude, and your appearance. Give your personal appearance careful attention. Dress your best, but not your flashiest. Choose conservative, appropriate clothing, and be sure it is immaculate. This is a business interview, and your appearance should indicate that you regard it as such. Besides, being well groomed and properly dressed will help boost your confidence.

Sooner or later, someone will call your name and escort you into the interview room. *This is it.* From here on you are on your own. It is too late for any more preparation. But remember, you asked for this opportunity to prove your fitness, and you are here because your request was granted.

What happens when you go in?

The usual sequence of events will be as follows: The clerk (who is often the board stenographer) will introduce you to the chairman of the oral board, who will introduce you to the other members of the board. Acknowledge the introductions before you sit down. Do not be surprised if you find a microphone facing you or a stenotypist sitting by. Oral interviews are usually recorded in the event of an appeal or other review.

Usually the chairman of the board will open the interview by reviewing the highlights of your education and work experience from your application – primarily for the benefit of the other members of the board, as well as to get the material into the record. Do not interrupt or comment unless there is an error or significant misinterpretation; if that is the case, do not hesitate. But do not quibble about insignificant matters. Also, he will usually ask you some question about your education, experience or your present job – partly to get you to start talking and to establish the interviewing "rapport." He may start the actual questioning, or turn it over to one of the other members. Frequently, each member undertakes the questioning on a particular area, one in which he is perhaps most competent, so you can expect each member to participate in the examination. Because time is limited, you may also expect some rather abrupt switches in the direction the questioning takes, so do not be upset by it. Normally, a board member will not pursue a single line of questioning unless he discovers a particular strength or weakness.

After each member has participated, the chairman will usually ask whether any member has any further questions, then will ask you if you have anything you wish to add. Unless you are expecting this question, it may floor you. Worse, it may start you off on an extended, extemporaneous speech. The board is not usually seeking more information. The question is principally to offer you a last opportunity to present further qualifications or to indicate that you have nothing to add. So, if you feel that a significant qualification or characteristic has been overlooked, it is proper to point it out in a sentence or so. Do not compliment the board on the thoroughness of their examination – they have been sketchy, and you know it. If you wish, merely say, "No thank you, I have nothing further to add." This is a point where you can "talk yourself out" of a good impression or fail to present an important bit of information. Remember, *you close the interview yourself.*

The chairman will then say, "That is all, Mr. _____, thank you." Do not be startled; the interview is over, and quicker than you think. Thank him, gather your belongings and take your leave. Save your sigh of relief for the other side of the door.

How to put your best foot forward

Throughout this entire process, you may feel that the board individually and collectively is trying to pierce your defenses, seek out your hidden weaknesses and embarrass and confuse you. Actually, this is not true. They are obliged to make an appraisal of your qualifications for the job you are seeking, and they want to see you in your best light. Remember, they must interview all candidates and a non-cooperative candidate may become a failure in spite of their best efforts to bring out his qualifications. Here are 15 suggestions that will help you:

1) Be natural – Keep your attitude confident, not cocky

If you are not confident that you can do the job, do not expect the board to be. Do not apologize for your weaknesses, try to bring out your strong points. The board is interested in a positive, not negative, presentation. Cockiness will antagonize any board member and make him wonder if you are covering up a weakness by a false show of strength.

2) Get comfortable, but don't lounge or sprawl

Sit erectly but not stiffly. A careless posture may lead the board to conclude that you are careless in other things, or at least that you are not impressed by the importance of the occasion. Either conclusion is natural, even if incorrect. Do not fuss with your clothing, a pencil or an ashtray. Your hands may occasionally be useful to emphasize a point; do not let them become a point of distraction.

3) Do not wisecrack or make small talk

This is a serious situation, and your attitude should show that you consider it as such. Further, the time of the board is limited – they do not want to waste it, and neither should you.

4) Do not exaggerate your experience or abilities
In the first place, from information in the application or other interviews and sources, the board may know more about you than you think. Secondly, you probably will not get away with it. An experienced board is rather adept at spotting such a situation, so do not take the chance.

5) If you know a board member, do not make a point of it, yet do not hide it
Certainly you are not fooling him, and probably not the other members of the board. Do not try to take advantage of your acquaintanceship – it will probably do you little good.

6) Do not dominate the interview
Let the board do that. They will give you the clues – do not assume that you have to do all the talking. Realize that the board has a number of questions to ask you, and do not try to take up all the interview time by showing off your extensive knowledge of the answer to the first one.

7) Be attentive
You only have 20 minutes or so, and you should keep your attention at its sharpest throughout. When a member is addressing a problem or question to you, give him your undivided attention. Address your reply principally to him, but do not exclude the other board members.

8) Do not interrupt
A board member may be stating a problem for you to analyze. He will ask you a question when the time comes. Let him state the problem, and wait for the question.

9) Make sure you understand the question
Do not try to answer until you are sure what the question is. If it is not clear, restate it in your own words or ask the board member to clarify it for you. However, do not haggle about minor elements.

10) Reply promptly but not hastily
A common entry on oral board rating sheets is "candidate responded readily," or "candidate hesitated in replies." Respond as promptly and quickly as you can, but do not jump to a hasty, ill-considered answer.

11) Do not be peremptory in your answers
A brief answer is proper – but do not fire your answer back. That is a losing game from your point of view. The board member can probably ask questions much faster than you can answer them.

12) Do not try to create the answer you think the board member wants
He is interested in what kind of mind you have and how it works – not in playing games. Furthermore, he can usually spot this practice and will actually grade you down on it.

13) Do not switch sides in your reply merely to agree with a board member
Frequently, a member will take a contrary position merely to draw you out and to see if you are willing and able to defend your point of view. Do not start a debate, yet do not surrender a good position. If a position is worth taking, it is worth defending.

14) Do not be afraid to admit an error in judgment if you are shown to be wrong

The board knows that you are forced to reply without any opportunity for careful consideration. Your answer may be demonstrably wrong. If so, admit it and get on with the interview.

15) Do not dwell at length on your present job

The opening question may relate to your present assignment. Answer the question but do not go into an extended discussion. You are being examined for a *new* job, not your present one. As a matter of fact, try to phrase ALL your answers in terms of the job for which you are being examined.

Basis of Rating

Probably you will forget most of these "do's" and "don'ts" when you walk into the oral interview room. Even remembering them all will not ensure you a passing grade. Perhaps you did not have the qualifications in the first place. But remembering them will help you to put your best foot forward, without treading on the toes of the board members.

Rumor and popular opinion to the contrary notwithstanding, an oral board wants you to make the best appearance possible. They know you are under pressure – but they also want to see how you respond to it as a guide to what your reaction would be under the pressures of the job you seek. They will be influenced by the degree of poise you display, the personal traits you show and the manner in which you respond.

ABOUT THIS BOOK

This book contains tests divided into Examination Sections. Go through each test, answering every question in the margin. We have also attached a sample answer sheet at the back of the book that can be removed and used. At the end of each test look at the answer key and check your answers. On the ones you got wrong, look at the right answer choice and learn. Do not fill in the answers first. Do not memorize the questions and answers, but understand the answer and principles involved. On your test, the questions will likely be different from the samples. Questions are changed and new ones added. If you understand these past questions you should have success with any changes that arise. Tests may consist of several types of questions. We have additional books on each subject should more study be advisable or necessary for you. Finally, the more you study, the better prepared you will be. This book is intended to be the last thing you study before you walk into the examination room. Prior study of relevant texts is also recommended. NLC publishes some of these in our Fundamental Series. Knowledge and good sense are important factors in passing your exam. Good luck also helps. So now study this Passbook, absorb the material contained within and take that knowledge into the examination. Then do your best to pass that exam.

EXAMINATION SECTION

EXAMINATION SECTION
TEST 1

DIRECTIONS: Each question or incomplete statement is followed by several suggested answers or completions. Select the one that BEST answers the question or completes the statement. *PRINT THE LETTER OF THE CORRECT ANSWER IN THE SPACE AT THE RIGHT.*

1. Two cleaners swept four corridors in 24 minutes. Each corridor measured 12 feet x 176 feet.
   The space swept per man per minute was MOST NEARLY _____ square feet.

   A. 50   B. 90   C. 180   D. 350

   1._____

2. The BEST time of the day to dust classroom furniture and woodwork is

   A. in the morning before the students arrive
   B. during the morning recess
   C. during the students' lunch time
   D. immediately after the students are dismissed for the day

   2._____

3. A custodian-engineer wishes to order sponges in the most economical manner. Keeping in mind that large sponges can be cut up into many smaller sizes, the one of the following that has the LEAST cost per cubic inch of sponge is

   A. 2" x 4" x 6" sponges @ $0.24
   B. 4" x 8" x 12" sponges @ $1.44
   C. 4" x 6" x 36" sponges @ $4.80
   D. 6" x 8" x 32" sponges @ $9.60

   3._____

4. Many new products are used in new schools for floors, walls, and other surfaces. A custodian-engineer should determine the BEST procedure to be used to clean such new surfaces by

   A. referring to the Board of Education's manual of procedures
   B. obtaining information on the cleaning procedure from the manufacturer
   C. asking the advice of the mechanics who installed the new material
   D. asking the district supervisor how to clean the surfaces

   4._____

5. The one of the following chemicals that a custodian-engineer should tell a cleaner to use to remove mildew from terazzo is

   A. ammonia   B. oxalic acid
   C. sodium hypochlorite   D. sodium silicate

   5._____

6. The type of soft floor that is basically a mixture of oxidized linseed oil, resin, and ground cork pressed upon a burlap backing is known as

   A. asphalt tile   B. cork tile
   C. linoleum   D. vinyl tile

   6._____

7. The difficulty of cleaning soil from surfaces is LEAST affected by the

   A. length of time between cleanings
   B. chemical nature of the soil

   7._____

C. smoothness of the surface being cleaned
D. standard time allotted to the job

8. The one of the following cleaning agents that is generally classified as an alkaline cleaner is

    A. sodium carbonate
    B. ground silica
    C. kerosene
    D. lemon oil

9. The one of the following cleaning agents that should be used ONLY when adequate ventilation and protective measures have been taken is

    A. methylene chloride
    B. sodium chloride
    C. sodium carbonate
    D. calcium carbonate

10. Of the following, the MOST important consideration in the selection of a cleaning agent is the

    A. cost per pound or gallon
    B. amount of labor involved in its use
    C. wording of the manufacturer's warranty
    D. length of time the manufacturer has been producing cleaning agents

11. The fan motor in a central vacuum cleaner system is found to be operating at 110% of its rated capacity.
The one of the following actions which is MOST likely to DECREASE the load on the motor is

    A. tying back several outlets in the open position on each floor
    B. moving the butterfly damper slightly toward the closed position
    C. removing ten percent of the filter bags
    D. operating the bag shaker continuously

12. The one of the following cleaning agents that should be used to remove an accumulation of grease from a concrete driveway is a(n)

    A. acid cleaner
    B. alkaline cleaner
    C. liquid soap
    D. solvent cleaner

13. The instructions for mixing a powdered cleaner in water state that you should mix three ounces of powder in a 14-quart pail three-quarters full of water.
To obtain a mixture of EQUAL strength in a mop truck containing 28 gallons of water requires _____ ounces of powder.

    A. 6   B. 8   C. 24   D. 32

14. A resin-base floor finish USUALLY

    A. gives the highest lustre of all floor finishes
    B. should be applied in one heavy coat
    C. provides a slip-resistant surface
    D. should not be used on asphalt tile

15. The one of the following cleaning operations of soft floors that generally requires MOST NEARLY the SAME amount of time per 1,000 square feet as damp mopping is   15._____

    A. applying a thin coat of wax
    B. sweeping
    C. dust mopping
    D. wet mopping

16. Of the following cleaning jobs, the one that should be allowed the MOST time to complete a 1,000 square foot area is   16._____

    A. vacuuming carpets
    B. washing painted walls
    C. stripping and waxing soft floors
    D. machine-scrubbing hard floors

17. Of the following, the MOST common use of sodium silicate is to   17._____

    A. seal concrete floors   B. condition leather
    C. treat boiler water   D. neutralize acid wastes

18. Cleaners should be instructed that dust mopping is LEAST appropriate for removing light soil from _____ floors.   18._____

    A. terrazzo floors   B. unsealed concrete
    C. resin-finished soft   D. sealed wood

19. Of the following, the substance that should be recommended for polishing hardwood furniture is   19._____

    A. lemon oil polish   B. neat's-foot oil
    C. paste wax   D. water-emulsion wax

20. The use of concentrated acid to remove stains from ceramic tile bathroom floors USUALLY results in making the surface   20._____

    A. pitted and porous   B. clean and shiny
    C. harder and glossier   D. waterproof

21. Asphalt tile floors should be protected by coating them with   21._____

    A. hard-milled soap   B. water-emulsion wax
    C. sodium metaphosphate   D. varnish

22. Of the following, the BEST way to economize on cleaning tools and materials is to   22._____

    A. train the cleaners to use them properly
    B. order at least a three-year supply of every item in order to avoid annual price increases
    C. attach a price sticker to every item so that the people using them will realize their high cost
    D. delay ordering material for three months at the beginning of each year to be sure that the old material is used to the fullest extent

23. The MINIMUM amount of free chlorine that swimming pool water should contain for proper disinfection is _____ parts per million.   23.____

    A. 1.0 B. 10 C. 50 D. 500

24. The point at which swimming pool filters should be back-washed is when the difference between the inlet and outlet pressures exceeds _____ psi.   24.____

    A. 5 B. 10 C. 15 D. 20

25. An orthtolidine test is used to test a water sample to see what quantity it contains of   25.____

    A. alum B. ammonia C. chlorine D. soda ash

26. The IDEAL flue gas temperature in a rotary-cup oil-fired boiler should be equal to the steam temperature plus   26.____

    A. 50° F B. 125° F C. 275° F D. 550° F

27. The carbon dioxide reading in a boiler flue when the boiler is operating efficiently should be MOST NEARLY   27.____

    A. 0.5 inches of water
    B. 8 ounces per mol
    C. 10 psi
    D. 12 percent

28. The one of the following that PRIMARILY indicates a low water level in a steam boiler is the   28.____

    A. pressure gauge
    B. gauge glass
    C. safety valve
    D. hydrometer

29. The one of the following steps that should be taken FIRST if a safety valve on a coal-fired steam boiler pops off is to   29.____

    A. add water to the boiler
    B. reduce the draft
    C. tap the side of the safety valve with a mallet
    D. open the bottom blow-off valve

30. A device that operates to vary the resistance of an electrical circuit is USUALLY part of a _____ pressurtrol.   30.____

    A. high-limit
    B. low-limit
    C. manual-reset
    D. modulating

KEY (CORRECT ANSWERS)

1.	C	16.	C
2.	A	17.	A
3.	B	18.	B
4.	B	19.	C
5.	C	20.	A
6.	C	21.	B
7.	D	22.	A
8.	A	23.	A
9.	A	24.	B
10.	B	25.	C
11.	B	26.	B
12.	D	27.	D
13.	D	28.	B
14.	C	29.	B
15.	A	30.	D

TEST 2

DIRECTIONS: Each question or incomplete statement is followed by several suggested answers or completions. Select the one that BEST answers the question or completes the statement. *PRINT THE LETTER OF THE CORRECT ANSWER IN THE SPACE AT THE RIGHT.*

1. A solenoid valve is actuated by

    A. air pressure
    B. electric current
    C. temperature change
    D. light rays

2. A sequential draft control on a rotary-cup oil-fired boiler should operate to

    A. *open* the automatic damper at the end of the post-purge period
    B. *open* the automatic damper when the draft has increased during normal burner operation
    C. *close* the automatic damper just before the burner motor starts up
    D. *close* the automatic damper after the burner goes off and the burner cycle is completed

3. The one of the following components of flue gas that indicates, when present, that more excess air is being supplied than is being used is

    A. carbon dioxide
    B. carbon monoxide
    C. nitrogen
    D. oxygen

4. An ADVANTAGE that a float-thermostatic steam trap has over a float-type steam trap of comparable rating is that a float-thermostatic trap

    A. requires less maintenance
    B. is easier to install
    C. allows non-condensable gases to escape
    D. releases the condensate at a higher temperature

5. A pump delivers 165 pounds of water per minute against a total head of 100 feet. The water horsepower of this pump is _____ HP.

    A. 1/2   B. 2   C. 5   D. 20

6. Of the following, the BEST instrument to use to measure over-the-fire draft is the

    A. Bourdon tube gauge
    B. inclined manometer
    C. mercury manometer
    D. potentiometer

7. The temperature of the water in a steam-heated domestic hot water tank is controlled by a(n)

    A. aquastat
    B. thermostatic regulating valve
    C. vacuum breaker
    D. thermostatic trap

8. The one of the following conditions that will MOST likely cause fuel oil pressure to fluctuate is

   A. a faulty pressure gauge
   B. a clean oil-strainer
   C. cold oil in the suction line
   D. an over-tight pump drive belt

9. The cooler in a Freon 12 refrigeration system that is equipped with automatic protective devices is MOST likely to be accidentally damaged by water freeze-up when the system('s)

   A. is operating at reduced load
   B. is operating at rated load
   C. condenser water-flow is interrupted
   D. is being pumped down

10. The capacity of a water-cooled condenser is LEAST affected by the

    A. water temperature
    B. refrigerant temperature
    C. surrounding air temperature
    D. quantity of condenser water being circulated

11. Of the following chemicals used in boiler feedwater treatment, the one that should be used to retard corrosion in the boiler circuit due to dissolved oxygen is sodium

    A. aluminate   B. carbonate   C. phosphate   D. sulfite

12. The heating system in a certain school is equipped with vacuum-return condensate pumps.
    The MOST likely place for an air-vent valve to be installed in this plant is on

    A. each radiator
    B. the outlet of the domestic hot-water steam heating coil
    C. the pressure side of the vacuum pump
    D. the shell of the domestic hot water tank

13. *Priming* of a steam boiler is NOT caused by

    A. load swings
    B. uneven fire distribution
    C. too high a water level
    D. high alkalinity of the boiled water

14. A Hartford loop is used in school heating systems PRIMARILY to

    A. provide for thermal expansion of the steam distribution piping
    B. equalize the water level in two or more boilers
    C. prevent siphoning of water out of the boiler
    D. by-pass the electric fuel-oil heaters when the steam heaters are operating

15. Of the following, the MOST likely use for temperature-indicating crayons by a custodian-engineer is in

   A. checking the operation of the radiator traps
   B. replacing room thermometers that have been vandalized
   C. indicating possible sources of spontaneous combustion
   D. checking the effectiveness of an insulating panel

16. A stop-and-waste cock is GENERALLY used on

   A. refrigerant lines between the compressor and the condenser
   B. soil lines
   C. gas supply lines
   D. water lines subjected to low temperatures

17. A pressure regulating valve in a compressed air line should be PRECEDED by a(n)

   A. check valve
   B. intercooler
   C. needle valve
   D. water-and-oil separator

18. A house trap is a fitting placed in the house drain immediately inside the foundation wall of a building.
The MAIN purpose of a house trap is to

   A. prevent the entrance of sewer gas into the building drainage system
   B. provide access to the drain lines in the basement for cleaning
   C. drain the basement in case of flooding
   D. maintain balanced air pressure in the fixture traps

19. The one of the following that is BEST to use to smooth a commutator is

   A. number 1/0 emery cloth
   B. number 00 sandpaper
   C. number 2 steel wool
   D. a safe edge file

20. The electric service that is provided to most schools in the city is nominally

   A. 208 volt-3 phase - 4 wire - 120 volts to ground
   B. 208 volt-3 phase - 3 wire - 208 volts to ground
   C. 220 volt-2 phase - 3 wire - 110 volts to ground
   D. 440 volt-3 phase - 4 wire - 240 volts to ground

21. All the fuses in an electrical panel are good but the clips on the fuse in circuit No. 1 are much hotter than the clips of the other fuses.
Of the following, the MOST likely cause of this condition is that

   A. circuit No. 1 is greatly overloaded
   B. circuit No. 1 is carrying much less than rated load
   C. the room temperature is abnormally high
   D. the fuse in circuit No. 1 is very loose in its clips

22. Of the following, the BEST tool to use to drive a lag screw is a(n)

   A. open-end wrench
   B. Stillson wrench
   C. screwdriver
   D. allen wrench

23. Of the following, the one that is MOST likely to be used in landscaping work as ground cover is

    A. barberry
    B. forsythia
    C. pachysandra
    D. viburnum

24. The velocity of air in a ventilation duct is USUALLY measured with a(n)

    A. hydrometer
    B. psychrometer
    C. pyrometer
    D. pitot tube

25. The motor driving a centrifugal pump through a direct-connected flexible coupling burned out.
    When a new motor is ordered, it is IMPORTANT to specify the same NEMA frame size so that the

    A. horsepower will be the same
    B. speed will be the same
    C. conduit box will be in the same location
    D. mounting dimensions will be the same

26. A custodian-engineer should inspect the school building for safety

    A. at least once each day
    B. at least every other day
    C. at least once a week
    D. at the end of each vacation period

27. Of the following, the MOST important practice to follow in order to prevent fires in a school is to train the staff to

    A. fight fires of every kind
    B. detect and eliminate every possible fire hazard
    C. keep halls, corridors, and exits clear
    D. place flammables in fire-proof container

28. The one of the following types of portable fire extinguishers that is MOST effective in fighting an oil fire is the _____ type.

    A. soda-acid
    B. loaded-stream
    C. foam
    D. carbon dioxide

29. A custodian-engineer opens the door to the boiler room and discovers that fuel oil has leaked onto the floor and caught fire.
    Of the following, the FIRST action he should take is to

    A. notify the principal
    B. notify the Fire Department
    C. turn off the remote control switch
    D. fight the fire using a Class B extinguisher

30. The MINIMUM noise level beyond which hearing may be impaired is _____ decibels.

    A. 10   B. 50   C. 90   D. 130

KEY (CORRECT ANSWERS)

1.	B	16.	D
2.	D	17.	D
3.	D	18.	A
4.	C	19.	B
5.	A	20.	A
6.	B	21.	D
7.	B	22.	A
8.	C	23.	C
9.	D	24.	D
10.	C	25.	D
11.	D	26.	A
12.	B	27.	B
13.	D	28.	C
14.	C	29.	C
15.	A	30.	C

EXAMINATION SECTION
TEST 1

DIRECTIONS: Each question or incomplete statement is followed by several suggested answers or completions. Select the one that BEST answers the question or completes the statement. *PRINT THE LETTER OF THE CORRECT ANSWER IN THE SPACE AT THE RIGHT.*

1. There are a considerable number of forms and reports to be submitted on schedule by a building custodian.
   The ADVISABLE method of accomplishing this duty is to

   A. fill out the reports at odd times during the days when you have free time
   B. schedule a definite period of the work week for completing these forms and reports
   C. assign your foreman or cleaner to handle all these forms for you and to have them available on time
   D. classify or group the forms and reports and fill out only one of each group and refer the other forms or reports to the ones completed

2. In enforcing compliance with safety regulations, you should take the attitude that they must be complied with because

   A. every accident can be prevented
   B. safety regulations are based on reason and experience with the best methods of accident prevention
   C. compliance with safety regulations will make other safety efforts unnecessary
   D. they are the law, and law enforcement is an end in itself

3. The use of trisodium phosphate in cleaning marble should be avoided because

   A. it discolors the surface of the marble
   B. the salt crystals get in the pores, expand, and crack the marble
   C. it pits the glazed surface and bleaches the marble
   D. it builds up a slick surface on the marble

4. The use of a concentrated cleaning solution on painted or varnished woodwork

   A. results in burning the pigments of paint or varnish, causing dull, streaky surfaces
   B. cuts down on time and energy in maintaining clean, unblemished surfaces
   C. insures spotless, clean, bright surfaces
   D. is detrimental to the health of the cleaners

5. A building custodian will make the BEST impression on the office staff if he

   A. impresses them with the importance of his job
   B. says little and is cold and distant
   C. is easy-going and good-natured
   D. is courteous and performs his duties with as little delay as possible

6. Domestic hot water storage reservoirs should be thoroughly cleaned once

   A. a week   B. a month
   C. a year   D. every two years

7. A *pH* value of 4 would indicate a(n)

   A. acid solution
   B. neutral solution
   C. alkaline solution
   D. low pressure heating system

8. When the diaphragm or bellows of a thermostatic radiator trap is found to be dirty, it is USUALLY cleaned with

   A. turpentine
   B. carbon tetrachloride
   C. kerosene
   D. mild soap and water

9. The CHIEF purpose of a plumbing trap is to

   A. permit air to enter the sewer
   B. prevent the entrance of sewer gas into the building
   C. break the shock of the water draining off
   D. siphon off the waste water

10. The safety device on the gas pilot flame of a gas-fired apparatus should operate on pilot flame failure to

    A. bypass the main gas supply directly to the flue
    B. switch over to auxiliary bottled gas pilot flame
    C. shut off the gas supply
    D. introduce sufficient excess air to keep the furnace below the lower explosive limit

11. When instructing employees in regard to their duties in case of fire, a supervisor should

    A. tell employees to take no action until the fire department equipment has arrived
    B. tell all employees to go to the scene of the fire
    C. assign each employee specific duties
    D. tell employees to extinguish the fire before calling the supervisor or the fire department

12. The PRINCIPAL value of a good report is that it

    A. is always available for reference
    B. impresses department heads with the need for immediate action
    C. reflects upon the writer of the report
    D. expedites official business

13. The quality of work performed by personnel engaged in building cleaning is BEST evaluated by

    A. studying building cleaning expenditures
    B. studying time records of personnel
    C. analyzing complaints by building occupants
    D. inspecting the building periodically

14. Of the following, a building custodian need NOT be kept informed on

    A. departmental management policies
    B. terms of union contracts covering his subordinates
    C. developments of current interest in custodial operations
    D. current rate of interest on municipal bonds

15. The BEST way to make work assignments to persons required to clean a multi-story building is to

    A. allow the persons to pick their room or area assignments out of a hat
    B. make specific room or area assignments to each person separately
    C. rotate room and area assignments daily according to a chart posted on the bulletin board
    D. each week let a different member of the group make the room or area assignment

16. One important use of accident reports is to provide information that may be used to reduce the possibility of similar accidents.
    The MOST valuable entry on the report for this purpose is the

    A. name of the victim
    B. injury sustained by the victim
    C. cause of the accident
    D. location of the accident

17. Suppose that an emergency has arisen which requires you to cancel some of the jobs scheduled for that day.
    Of the following jobs, the one that can be eliminated for that day with LEAST effect on the proper operation and maintenance of the building is

    A. mopping and cleaning toilet rooms
    B. checking public stairs and corridors for hazards
    C. improving the location of supplies in the storeroom
    D. replacing broken window panes in offices

18. Of the following, a building custodian's attitude toward grievances should be to

    A. pay little attention to little grievances
    B. be very alert to grievances and make adjustments in existing conditions to appease all of them
    C. know the most frequent causes of grievances and strive to prevent them from arising
    D. maintain rigid discipline of a nature that *smoothes out* all grievances

19. A heavy snowfall must be removed from the sidewalks around the building. You, as building custodian, have assigned two men to shovel snow from the walks. After an interval, you check and find they are bickering as to how much each is shoveling, and no snow is being removed.
    In this situation, you should

    A. stand with them to supervise the snow removal and to be sure the work is divided evenly
    B. assign two other men to snow removal and send the original two back to their usual chores
    C. put the man with seniority in full charge of the other man
    D. separate the men by sending them to opposite ends of the walks to shovel alone, with a warning that you will be checking on their progress at short intervals

20. Of the following, safety on the job is BEST assured by 20.____
    A. keeping alert
    B. following every rule
    C. working very slowly
    D. never working alone

KEY (CORRECT ANSWERS)

1.	B	11.	C
2.	B	12.	D
3.	B	13.	D
4.	A	14.	D
5.	D	15.	B
6.	C	16.	C
7.	A	17.	C
8.	C	18.	C
9.	B	19.	D
10.	C	20.	A

TEST 2

DIRECTIONS: Each question or incomplete statement is followed by several suggested answers or completions. Select the one that BEST answers the question or completes the statement. *PRINT THE LETTER OF THE CORRECT ANSWER IN THE SPACE AT THE RIGHT.*

1. A foam-type fire extinguisher extinguishes fires by

    A. cooling *only*
    B. drenching *only*
    C. smothering *only*
    D. cooling and smothering

    1.____

2. The extinguishing agent in a soda-acid fire extinguisher is

    A. carbon dioxide
    B. water
    C. carbon tetrachloride
    D. calcium chloride solution

    2.____

3. The PROPER extinguisher to use on an electrical fire in an operating electric motor is

    A. foam
    B. carbon dioxide
    C. soda and acid
    D. water

    3.____

4. When an extension ladder is in place and ready to be used, the rope used to extend the ladder should be

    A. left hanging free out of the way of the climber's feet
    B. used to raise and lower tools to the man on the ladder
    C. used as a means of steadying the climber
    D. tied securely around a lower rung

    4.____

5. The PRINCIPAL characteristic of panic locks or bolts on doors of places of public assembly is that they

    A. allow the doors to open outwardly with sufficient pressure on the bars of the lock
    B. allow the doors to open inwardly with sufficient pressure on the bars of the lock
    C. prevent the door from opening under impact load
    D. may be opened with any tumbler lock key

    5.____

6. The MAIN purpose of periodic inspections and tests of electrical equipment is to

    A. encourage the men to take better care of the equipment
    B. make the men familiar with the equipment
    C. discover minor faults before they develop into major faults
    D. keep the men busy during otherwise slack periods

    6.____

7. Standard, extra strong, and double extra strong welded steel pipe of a given size all have the SAME

    A. outside diameter
    B. inside diameter
    C. average diameter
    D. flow capacity for any given flow velocity

    7.____

8. In reference to domestic gas piping,

   A. couplings with running threads are used to join pipes
   B. risers must have a drip leg and cap at bottom
   C. gasketed unions may be used in joining pipe
   D. composition disc globe valves are used to throttle the gas

9. Chewing gum should be removed from rubber, asphalt, or linoleum flooring with

   A. a putty knife   B. steel wool
   C. gritty compounds   D. a solvent

10. Which one of the following is the BEST procedure to follow when the linoleum floor of a meeting room containing movable furniture is to be mopped?

    A. The furniture should be moved by sliding it along the floor to prevent injury to the cleaners.
    B. The furniture should not be moved.
    C. The furniture should be moved by lifting it and carrying it to a clear spot to prevent damage to the linoleum.
    D. Very little water should be used in order to prevent the legs of the furniture from getting wet.

11. Asphalt tile flooring that has been subjected to oily compounds

    A. may last indefinitely
    B. must be removed and replaced with new asphalt tile immediately
    C. may be restored to hardness and lustre by several moppings with hot water and several applications of water wax
    D. must be restored to original condition by several moppings with kerosene

12. The use of alcohol in water for washing windows is NOT recommended because it

    A. is a hazard to the cleaner in that he may be affected by the fumes
    B. will damage the paint around the edges of the glass
    C. pits the surface of the glass
    D. destroys the bristles of the brush applying the solution to the pane

13. Of the following, the BEST material to use for removing grass stains on marble or wood is

    A. oxalic acid   B. chloride of lime
    C. sodium silicate   D. sodium hypochlorite

14. Shades or Venetian blinds are PREFERABLY cleaned with a

    A. feather duster   B. counter brush
    C. damp sponge   D. vacuum cleaner

15. Asphalt tile floors are PREFERABLY polished with

    A. water emulsion wax   B. wax in solution with benzol
    C. a high fatty acid soap D. sodium metaphosphate

16. Washing soda is used to   16._____

    A. eliminate the need for rinse mopping or wiping
    B. make the cleaning compound abrasive
    C. decrease the wetting power of water
    D. increase the wetting power of water

17. Varnish or lacquer may be used as a sealer on floors finished with   17._____

    A. asphalt tiles   B. linoleum
    C. rubber tiles   D. cork tiles

18. A long-handled deck scrub brush is MOST effective when scrubbing   18._____

    A. large open areas   B. stair treads
    C. small flat areas   D. long corridors

19. The BEST method for preventing the infestation of a building by rats is to   19._____

    A. use cats
    B. use rat traps
    C. eliminate rat harborages in the building
    D. use poisoned bait

20. The one of the following foodstuffs which, if allowed to remain on ordinary asphalt tile, will MOST likely be most injurious to it is   20._____

    A. milk   B. maple syrup
    C. ketchup   D. salad oil

KEY (CORRECT ANSWERS)

1.	D	11.	C
2.	B	12.	B
3.	B	13.	D
4.	D	14.	D
5.	A	15.	A
6.	C	16.	D
7.	A	17.	D
8.	B	18.	C
9.	A	19.	C
10.	C	20.	D

TEST 3

DIRECTIONS: Each question or incomplete statement is followed by several suggested answers or completions. Select the one that BEST answers the question or completes the statement. *PRINT THE LETTER OF THE CORRECT ANSWER IN THE SPACE AT THE RIGHT.*

1. Employees engaged in cleaning operations who are issued rubber gloves to protect their hands against caustic solutions should be warned that

    A. such solution allowed to spill over the glove top into the space between the glove and the hand may damage the skin of the hand
    B. rubber gloves have a very short life in contact with caustic solutions
    C. harmful gases can penetrate the rubber and harm even dry hands
    D. contact of the hands with glove-type rubber for over an hour is harmful

    1.____

2. Pyrethrins are used as

    A. insecticides   B. germicides
    C. waxes   D. detergents

    2.____

3. Water hammer is

    A. a special hammer used to remove scale from a radiator
    B. caused by water in steam lines
    C. caused by excessive boiler pressure
    D. caused by low water level in the boiler

    3.____

4. Which of the following is USUALLY used in the construction of a steam pressure gauge?

    A. Perfect circle tube   B. Venturi tube
    C. Bourdon tube   D. Elastic linkage

    4.____

5. Usually when a large room is gradually filled with people, the room temperature

    A. and humidity both decrease
    B. increases and the humidity decreases
    C. and humidity increase
    D. decreases and humidity increases

    5.____

6. A foot valve at the intake end of the suction line of a pump serves MAINLY to

    A. maintain pump prime
    B. filter out large particles in the fluid
    C. increase the maximum suction lift of the pump
    D. increase pump flow rate

    6.____

7. A pressure gauge attached to a standpipe system shows a pressure of 36 pounds per sq. in.
The head of water, in feet, above the gauge is MOST NEARLY

    A. 24   B. 36   C. 60   D. 83

    7.____

8. Of the following, the term *vapor barrier* would MOST likely be associated with

    A. electric service installation
    B. insulation materials
    C. fuel oil tank installation
    D. domestic gas piping

9. Pitot tubes are used to

    A. test feed water for impurities
    B. measure air or gas flow in a duct
    C. prevent overheating of elements of a steam gauge
    D. control the ignition system of an oil burner

10. In warm air heating and in ventilating systems, laboratories and kitchens should NOT be equipped with return ducts in order to

    A. keep air velocities in other returns as high as possible
    B. reduce fire hazards
    C. reduce the possibility of circulating odors through the system
    D. keep the temperature high in these rooms

11. One square foot of equivalent direct steam radiation (EDR) is equivalent to a heat emission of _____ BTU per _____.

    A. 150; hour   B. 240; minute
    C. 150; minute   D. 240; hour

12. Of the following, the one which is LEAST likely to cause continuous vibration of an operating motor is

    A. a faulty starting circuit
    B. excessive belt tension
    C. the misalignment of motor and driven equipment
    D. loose bearings

13. The function of a steam trap is to

    A. remove sediment and dirt from steam
    B. remove air and non-condensible gases from steam
    C. relieve excessive steam pressure to the atmosphere
    D. remove condensate from a pipe or an apparatus

14. The temperature at which air is just saturated with the moisture present in it is called its

    A. relative humidity   B. absolute humidity
    C. humid temperature   D. dew point

15. If scale forms on the seat of a float-operated boiler feed water regulator, the MOST likely result is

    A. internal corrosion of the boiler shell
    B. insufficient supply of water to the boiler
    C. flooding of the boiler
    D. shutting down of the oil burner by the low water cut-out

16. The compound gauge in the oil suction line shows a high vacuum. This is USUALLY an indication of

    A. a dirty oil strainer
    B. low oil level in the fuel oil storage tank
    C. a leak in the fuel oil preheater
    D. an obstruction in the fuel oil preheater

17. Of the following, the information which is LEAST important on a boiler room log sheet is the

    A. stack temperature readings
    B. CO_2 readings
    C. number of boilers in operation
    D. boiler room humidity

18. Pitting and corrosion of the water side of the boiler heating surfaces is due MAINLY to the boiler water containing dissolved

    A. oxygen   B. hydrogen
    C. soda-ash   D. sodium sulphite

19. The combustion efficiency of a boiler can be determined with a CO_2

    A. flue gas temperature   B. boiler room humidity
    C. outside air temperature   D. under fire draft

20. The try-cocks of steam boilers are used to

    A. find the height of water in the boiler
    B. test steam pressure in the boiler
    C. empty the boiler of water
    D. act as safety valves

KEY (CORRECT ANSWERS)

1.	A	11.	D
2.	A	12.	A
3.	B	13.	D
4.	C	14.	D
5.	C	15.	C
6.	A	16.	A
7.	D	17.	D
8.	B	18.	A
9.	B	19.	A
10.	C	20.	A

TEST 4

DIRECTIONS: Each question or incomplete statement is followed by several suggested answers or completions. Select the one that BEST answers the question or completes the statement. *PRINT THE LETTER OF THE CORRECT ANSWER IN THE SPACE AT THE RIGHT.*

1. The reason for sweating inside a refrigerator cabinet is   1.____

   A. high percent running time of compressor unit
   B. high cabinet air temperature
   C. defective expansion valve
   D. a poor door seal

2. Of the following ingredients, the ones to be mixed with water to *point-up* the brickwork of   2.____
   a building are: 1 part cement,

   A. 2 parts sand, 3 parts gravel
   B. 3 parts sand, 4 parts gravel
   C. 3 parts sand
   D. 5 parts sand

3. Acid soils can BEST be neutralized by liberal applications of   3.____

   A. manure   B. salt
   C. lime   D. powdered-basalt

4. Summer blooming flower bulbs should be stored in a _____ place.   4.____

   A. warm, dry   B. warm, moist
   C. cool, moist   D. cool, dry

5. A certain 31-day month had an average temperature of 45 Fahrenheit.   5.____
   The number of degree days for this month is

   A. 31   B. 450   C. 620   D. 1395

6. While concrete is *curing*, it is MOST desirable to   6.____

   A. expose the concrete to sun and air as much as possible
   B. keep the concrete surface moist
   C. maintain a temperature of not more than 60°F
   D. maintain a temperature of at least 80°F

7. To join two lengths of pipe together in a solid straight run, the fitting to use is a   7.____

   A. coupling   B. tee
   C. hickey   D. shoulder nipple

8. New copper flashing that has been soldered should be   8.____

   A. muriatic acid   B. plain water
   C. benzine   D. washing soda or lye

9. The intercooler of a two-stage air compressor is connected to the compressor between the

   A. two stages
   B. filter and the first stage
   C. second stage and the receiver
   D. receiver and point of usage of the air

9.____

10. Both terms *tank* and *close* apply USUALLY to

    A. electric generator couplings
    B. freon storage units
    C. pipe nipples
    D. ventilation plenum chambers

10.____

11. The commercial fertilizer *5-10-5* refers to

    A. 5% nitrogen, 10% phosphoric acid, 5% potash
    B. 5% rotted manure, 10% calcium chloride, 5% bone meal
    C. 5% soda, 10% tobacco dust, 5% bone meal
    D. 5% tobacco dust, 10% rotted manure, 5% sulphur

11.____

12. The slope or slant of a soil line is 1/4" per foot. If this drainage line is 50' long, the difference in elevation from one end to the other is, in feet, MOST NEARLY

    A. 0.55   B. 1.04   C. 2.08   D. 12.5

12.____

13. Oil is used with sharpening stones when sharpening wood chisels in order to

    A. reduce the effort needed to move the blade over the stone
    B. maintain the oil temper of the steel used for the chisel
    C. flush off the small metal chips and clear the cutting edges of the abrasive grit
    D. reduce the temperature due to friction

13.____

14. A maintenance man checking a refrigerator for a freon leak would use a

    A. soap and water solution
    B. halide torch
    C. glycerine solution
    D. linseed oil and whiting solution

14.____

15. A basement floor area of 5000 square feet is under 9 inches of water.
    If this 9 inches of water is to be pumped out of the basement in one hour, the required capacity of the portable pump, in gallons per minute, is MOST NEARLY

    A. 63   B. 470   C. 1020   D. 2810

15.____

16. A MAJOR advantage of keeping a perpetual inventory of supplies is that it

    A. gives a current record of the supplies available at all times
    B. reduces the work required to distribute supplies
    C. avoids the need for periodic physical inventories
    D. shows who is using excessive supplies

16.____

17. Employees generally do NOT object to strict rules and regulations if they

   A. are enforced without bias or favor
   B. result in more material gain
   C. deal with relatively unimportant phases of the work
   D. affect the supervisors more than their subordinates

18. In order to have building employees willing to follow standardized cleaning and maintenance procedures, the supervisor MUST be prepared to

   A. work alongside the employees
   B. demonstrate the reasonableness of the procedures
   C. offer incentive pay for their use
   D. be adamant in opposing changes in the standardized procedures

19. Of the following, the MOST important step when accepting incoming shipments of standard items normally carried in stock is to check the items for

   A. electrical performance
   B. chemical composition
   C. quantity delivered
   D. mechanical performance

20. The orderly arrangement of supplies in storage USUALLY

   A. takes too much time to be worthwhile
   B. is important only in large warehouses
   C. is essential for stock selection and inventory purposes
   D. cannot be accomplished when package sizes vary

KEY (CORRECT ANSWERS)

1.	D	11.	A
2.	C	12.	B
3.	C	13.	C
4.	D	14.	B
5.	C	15.	B
6.	B	16.	A
7.	A	17.	A
8.	D	18.	B
9.	A	19.	C
10.	C	20.	C

EXAMINATION SECTION
TEST 1

DIRECTIONS: Each question or incomplete statement is followed by several suggested answers or completions. Select the one that BEST answers the question or completes the statement. *PRINT THE LETTER OF THE CORRECT ANSWER IN THE SPACE AT THE RIGHT.*

1. Of the following, the PREFERRED sequence of tasks to be followed in office cleaning is   1.____

    A. dust desks, empty ash trays and waste baskets, mop floor
    B. mop floor, dust desks, empty ash trays and waste baskets
    C. empty ash trays and waste baskets, dust desks, mop floor
    D. mop floor, empty ash trays and waste baskets, dust desks

2. When vacuum cleaning rugs, the suction tool should be pushed   2.____

    A. diagonally across the lay of the nap
    B. with the lay of the nap
    C. across the lay of the nap
    D. against the lay of the nap

3. The brownish discoloration that sometimes occurs in hot water circulating systems is USUALLY due to   3.____

    A. molds   B. algae   C. bacteria   D. rust

4. The type of valve that does NOT have a stuffing or packing gland is a _____ valve.   4.____

    A. globe   B. radiator   C. check   D. gate

5. Assuming that the hot and cold water demand of a fixture will be the same, then the normal size of the hot water pipe with respect to that of the cold water pipe should be   5.____

    A. the same
    B. twice as great
    C. one and one-half times as great
    D. one half as great

6. If the pitch of a horizontal steam line is 1/2 inch in 10 feet, one end of a 45-foot steam line is lower than the other end by, MOST NEARLY, _____ inches.   6.____

    A. 2   B. 2 1/4   C. 3   D. 3 1/2

7. A pump that removes 30 gallons of water per minute is pumping water from a cellar 30 feet x 50 feet covered with eight inches of water. One cubic foot of water equals 7.5 gallons of water.
The number of minutes it will take to remove the eight inches of water from the cellar is, MOST NEARLY,   7.____

    A. 200   B. 225   C. 250   D. 275

8. Oil preheaters are used to   8.____

    A. economize on fuel oil
    B. reduce friction in the oil blower
    C. improve the flow of oil
    D. reduce oil volatility

25

9. The FIRST item which should be checked when a sump pit overflows because the automatic electric sump pump is not operating properly is the

   A. feedwater pressure
   B. ficat switch mechanism
   C. stat switch
   D. discharge line check valve

10. Chloride of lime should be used for the removal of

    A. alkali stains on wood
    B. grass stains on wood or marble
    C. indelible pencil and marking ink stains on concrete or terrazzo
    D. ink stains on wood

11. Of the following, the lack of a vapor barrier on the inside surface of a well-insulated wall may eventually cause, during the winter,

    A. plugging of weep holes
    B. peeling of exterior paint
    C. lower heat losses through the wall
    D. improvement in insulation performance by plugging air spaces with the insulation

12. When cold water pipes in a room *sweat*, it is USUALLY due to the

    A. surface of the pipes being below the dew point temperature of the room air
    B. specific humidity exceeding the relative humidity
    C. air in the room exceeding 100% relative humidity
    D. surface of the pipe being below the wet bulb temperature of the room air

13. The MAIN reason for applying floor finish to a floor surface is to

    A. protect against germs
    B. protect the floor surface
    C. increase traction
    D. waterproof the floor

14. The MAIN reason for preventing sewer gas from entering buildings through the plumbing system is because the gas

    A. is highly inflammable and explosive in nature and could result in a fire hazard
    B. has an eroding effect on plumbing fixtures and pipe lines
    C. is highly infectious and contagious in nature
    D. has a nuisance effect on occupants

15. The one of the following that is a concrete floor sealer is

    A. sodium silicate
    B. neatsfoot oil
    C. sodium hydroxide
    D. linseed oil

16. To help plants survive the shock of transplanting, in most cases, it is BEST to

    A. spray them with insecticide every day for a week
    B. cover the foliage with burlap for a day or two
    C. shade them from the sun for a week or two
    D. prune them every day for a week or two

17. When cutting a branch off a tree, it is desirable to undercut because it will   17._____

    A. prevent the weight of the branch from tearing off bark and wood below the cut
    B. make the tree grow stronger and straighter
    C. let the saw work smoother and easier
    D. make it easier to cut up the limb

18. The *MAIN* reason for applying lime to soil is to control its   18._____

    A. aridity   B. fertilization
    C. acidity   D. porosity

19. The *GREATEST* danger to a tree from a large unprotected wound is that   19._____

    A. birds may build a nest in it
    B. the tree may bleed to death
    C. the wound may become infected
    D. it is open to the elements

20. The fertilizer that is used for the care of trees should have a high content of   20._____

    A. DDT   B. nitrogen   C. sulphur   D. carbon

21. The area of the plot plan shown below is _____ square feet.   21._____

    A. 25,300
    B. 26,700
    C. 28,100
    D. 30,500

22. The *BEST* of the following combinations of instruments to use in checking the combustion efficiency of a heating boiler is   22._____

    A. anemometer, stack thermometer, and orsat apparatus
    B. draft gage, psychrometer, and barometer
    C. draft gage, stack thermometer, and orsat apparatus
    D. draft gage, stack thermometer, and barometer

23. The one of the following that does NOT indicate low water in a steam boiler is the   23._____

    A. fusible plug   B. safety valve
    C. tri cocks   D. gauge glass

24. The increase in the stack temperature toward the end of the heating system above what it was at the beginning of the season is an indication that the   24._____

    A. radiators and convectors are air bound
    B. tubes and heating surfaces of the boiler are becoming insulated with soot
    C. furnace fire brick is failing
    D. heat content of the fuel is improving

25. Of the following, the one which is NOT a general class of oil burners is the _____ atomizing.

    A. water   B. rotary cup   C. mechanical   D. air

26. Of the following, the one which should be between a boiler and its safety valve is

    A. a swing check valve of a size larger than that of the safety valve
    B. a butterfly valve located in the boiler-nozzle
    C. a gate valve of the same nominal size as that of the safety valve
    D. no valve of any type

27. The term *spinner cup* refers to

    A. screw-type stokers   B. gun-type oil burners
    C. rotary-type oil burners   D. chain grate stokers

28. A *gun-type* burner is often used on a

    A. pot-type oil burner
    B. low pressure gas boiler
    C. coal underfeed stoker boiler
    D. high pressure oil-fired boiler

29. Of the following, the action that should be taken as the FIRST step if a properly adjusted safety valve on a steam boiler *pops off* when in operation is

    A. open the-draft   B. add more water to the boiler
    C. wire the valve shut   D. reduce the draft

30. When the water gets below the safe level in an operating boiler, it is BEST to

    A. add new water up to the safe level and open up the fire so that the water will heat quickly
    B. check the fire and let the boiler cool down before new water is added
    C. add new water to the boiler immediately
    D. check the fire and empty the boiler

31. Vents on fuel oil storage tanks are used to

    A. fill the fuel tanks
    B. allow air to escape during filling
    C. check oil flash points
    D. make tank fuel soundings

32. Of the following, the MOST desirable way to remove carbon deposits from the atomizing cup of an oil burner is to

    A. apply a hot flame to the carbonized surfaces to burn off the carbon deposits
    B. use kerosene to loosen the deposits and wipe with a soft cloth
    C. wash the cup with a mild trisodium phosphate solution and dry with a cloth
    D. use a scraper, followed by light rubbing with emery cloth

33. Of the following, the MOST important precaution that should be taken when *cutting in* a boiler in a battery is to see that the 33.____

    A. water column is at least 1 inch below top row of tubes
    B. non-return valve is closed when the boiler pressure is rising
    C. safety valves function properly
    D. boiler pressure is about equal to header pressure

34. A condensate feedwater tank in a low pressure steam plant 34.____

    A. is hermetically sealed to prevent contamination of feed water
    B. contains a surface blow down line
    C. is vented to the atmosphere
    D. has a vacuum breaker exposed to the atmosphere

35. Of the following, the FIRST action to take in the event a low pressure steam boiler gauge glass breaks is to 35.____

    A. bank the fires
    B. close the water gauge glass cocks
    C. open the safety valve
    D. blow down the boiler

36. A *barometric damper* would be used in a boiler installation fired under draft conditions that are called 36.____

    A. induced   B. natural   C. regenerate   D. forced

37. The flue gas temperature, when firing oil, should be just high enough to evaporate any contained moisture in order to 37.____

    A. prevent an acid from forming and eroding the breeching
    B. decrease the amount of excess air needed
    C. prevent an air pollution condition
    D. lower the combustion efficiency of the boiler

38. A compound gauge in a boiler room 38.____

    A. measures pressures above and below atmospheric pressure
    B. indicates the degree of compounding in a steam engine
    C. shows the quantity of boiler treatment compound on hand
    D. measures steam and water pressure

39. In the combustion of the common fuels, the PRINCIPAL boiler heat loss is that due to the heat 39.____

    A. carried away by the moisture in the fuel
    B. lost by radiation
    C. carried away by the flue gases
    D. lost by incomplete combustion

40. Of the following, the CORRECT sequence of steps to use when removing a boiler from service in order to perform extensive repairs on it is   40._____
    A. discontinue firing, drain boiler, turn off valves, cool boiler
    B. discontinue firing, drain boiler, turn off valves
    C. turn off valves, drain boiler, discontinue firing, cool boiler
    D. discontinue firing, turn off valves, cool boiler, drain boiler

---

KEY (CORRECT ANSWERS)

1.	C	11.	B	21.	C	31.	B
2.	B	12.	A	22.	C	32.	B
3.	D	13.	B	23.	B	33.	D
4.	C	14.	D	24.	B	34.	C
5.	A	15.	A	25.	A	35.	B
6.	B	16.	C	26.	D	36.	B
7.	C	17.	A	27.	C	37.	A
8.	C	18.	C	28.	D	38.	A
9.	B	19.	C	29.	D	39.	C
10.	C	20.	B	30.	B	40.	D

TEST 2

DIRECTIONS: Each question or incomplete statement is followed by several suggested answers or completions. Select the one that BEST answers the question or completes the statement. *PRINT THE LETTER OF THE CORRECT ANSWER IN THE SPACE AT THE RIGHT.*

1. With the same outdoor winter temperatures, the load on a heating boiler starting up is greater than the normal morning load MAINLY because of

    A. loss of heat escaping through the stack
    B. steam required to heat boiler water and piping to radiators
    C. viscosity of the fuel oil
    D. low outdoor temperatures

2. The FIRST operation when starting a boiler after it has been on bank overnight should be to

    A. blow down the boiler
    B. clean the furnace
    C. check the gate valves
    D. look at the water gauge and try the gauge cocks

3. *Cascading* of raw city water when filling a cleaned boiler should be avoided because it

    A. is harmful to the mud drum
    B. adds additional free oxygen in the boiler
    C. adds considerable time to the filling procedure
    D. will stress tube and sheet joints

4. The average temperature on a day in January was 24° F. The number of degree-days for that day was

    A. 12 B. 24 C. 41 D. 48

5. Under normal conditions during the growing season, lawns should receive a good saturation of water with a spray

    A. once a day
    B. once a week
    C. once a month
    D. twice a month

6. One of the important benefits to floors that wax does NOT provide is

    A. easier soil removal
    B. improved stain resistance
    C. reduction in wear
    D. resistance to fire

7. In the Ringelmann chart of smoke density, number 4 indicates

    A. the darkest smoke condition
    B. the lightest smoke condition
    C. smoke density of 80 per cent
    D. no smoke condition

8. Of the following, the estinguishing agent that should be used on fires in flammable liquids is

   A. steam   B. water   C. foam   D. soda and acid

9. A soda-acid fire extinguisher is recommended for use on fires consisting of

   A. wood or paper
   B. fuel oil or gasoline
   C. electrical causes or fuel oil
   D. paint or turpentine

10. The CHIEF reason wooden ladders should NOT be painted is that the paint may

    A. hide defects
    B. mark up the walls
    C. make the ladder slippery
    D. damage the rungs

11. In accordance with the uniform method of identifying piping in public buildings, pipes carrying materials classified as being dangerous are colored

    A. blue
    B. red
    C. orange and yellow
    D. green and white

12. The MOST effective way to eliminate fire hazards in public buildings is to

    A. hold frequent fire drills
    B. have the fire department inspect the building annually
    C. promote constant self-inspection
    D. supply each building with ample fire fighting equipment

13. When a room is air conditioned in the summer, the windows should be

    A. opened at the top and bottom to improve circulation
    B. screened to keep out the dirt
    C. kept closed
    D. opened at the top only to let hot air escape

14. In order to clean an office with 20,000 sq. ft. of space in four hours, using a standard of 900 sq. ft. per hour, the number of cleaners you should assign to do the job is MOST NEARLY

    A. 4   B. 6   C. 8   D. 10

15. The area of a floor 35' wide and 45' long is, in square yards, MOST NEARLY

    A. 175   B. 262   C. 525   D. 1575

16. A pyrometer is an instrument used for measuring

    A. condensation and humidity
    B. high temperatures
    C. noise pollution
    D. water flow

17. It is usually desirable to assign the cleaning of an office to one employee only because   17._____

    A. the amount of time wasted through talking is decreased
    B. an employee working alone, by himself, is more efficient
    C. there is no question who is responsible for the work done
    D. working alone reduces the rate and severity of accidents

18. Of each dollar spent on the cleaning of public buildings, the amount spent on cleaning   18._____
    supplies is usually not more than _____ cents.

    A. 5   B. 35   C. 55   D. 75

19. Of the following solutions, the one MOST often used in washing exterior glass is _____   19._____
    water and a small quantity of _____.

    A. cold; turpentine   B. cold; ammonia
    C. cold; glass wax   D. warm; soft soap

20. Rust stains in wash basins can BEST be prevented by   20._____

    A. applying wax film to the rusty surface
    B. replacing leaking faucet washers
    C. adding rust inhibitor to the domestic cold water storage tank
    D. sand papering the rusty surfaces

21. Of the following, the one which is likely to be MOST harmful to asphalt tile is   21._____

    A. coffee   B. ketchup   C. salad oil   D. vinegar

22. Of the following, when sweeping a corridor with a floor brush, the cleaner should   22._____

    A. lean on the brush and walk the length of the corridor
    B. give the brush a slight jerk after each stroke to free it of loose dirt
    C. make certain there is no overlap on sweeping strokes
    D. use moderately long pull strokes

23. Time standards for cleaning are of value ONLY if   23._____

    A. a bonus is promised if the time standards are beaten
    B. the cleaners determine the methods and procedures to be used
    C. accompanied by a completely detailed description of the methods to be used
    D. a schematic diagram of the area is made available to the cleaners

24. Of the following, the one which is the LEAST important factor in deciding that additional   24._____
    training is necessary for the men you supervise is that

    A. the quality of work is below standard
    B. supplies are being wasted
    C. too much time is required to do specific jobs
    D. the absentee rate has declined

25. To promote proper safety practices in the operation of power tools and equipment, you   25._____
    should emphasize in meetings with the staff that

    A. every accident can be prevented through proper safety regulations
    B. proper safety practices will probably make future safety meetings unnecessary

C. when safety rules are followed, tools and equipment will work better
D. safety rules are based on past experience with the best methods of preventing accidents

26. A good practical method to use in determining whether an employee is doing his job properly is to

    A. assume that if he asks no questions, he knows the work
    B. question him directly on details of the job
    C. inspect and follow up the work which is assigned to him
    D. ask other employees how this employee is making out

27. If an employee continually asks how he should do his work, you should

    A. dismiss him immediately
    B. pretend you do not hear him unless he persists
    C. explain the work carefully but encourage him to use his own judgment
    D. tell him not to ask so many questions

28. You have instructed an employee to wet-mop a certain area. To be sure that the employee understands the instructions you have given him, you should

    A. ask him to repeat the instructions to you
    B. check with him after he has done the job
    C. watch him while he is doing the job
    D. repeat the instructions to the employee

29. One of your men disagrees with your evaluation of his work.
    Of the following, the BEST way to handle this situation would be to

    A. explain that you are in a better position to evaluate his work than he is
    B. tell him that since other men are satisfied with your evaluation, he should accept their opinions
    C. explain the basis of your evaluation and discuss it with him
    D. refuse to discuss his complaint in order to maintain discipline

30. Of the following, the one which is NOT a quality of leadership desirable in a supervisor is

    A. intelligence   B. integrity
    C. forcefulness   D. partiality

31. Of the following, the one which LEAST characterizes the *grapevine* is that it

    A. consists of a tremendous amount of rumor, conjecture, information, advice, prediction, and even orders
    B. seems to rise spontaneously, is largely anonymous, spreads rapidly, and changes in unpredictable directions
    C. can be eliminated without any great effort
    D. commonly fills the gaps left by the regular organizational channels of communication

32. Of the following, the one which is NOT a purpose of a cleaning job breakdown is to

    A. eliminate unnecessary steps
    B. determine the type of floor wax to use

C. rearrange the sequence of operations to save time
D. combine steps or actions where practicable

33. Of the following, the PRINCIPAL function of a supervisor is to

    A. train and instruct his subordinates in the proper methods of doing their work
    B. eliminate all accidents
    C. prepare reports on his activities to his supervisor
    D. prepare a thorough job methods analysis

34. The BEST method of making cleaning assignments in a large building is by means of

    A. daily rotation
    B. specific assignment
    C. individual choice
    D. chronological order

35. When one of your new cleaning employees is making little progress after the usual training period with one of your experienced men, you should

    A. recommend to your superior that he should be discharged
    B. tell your superior he is not interested in the job
    C. determine the reason for the poor results
    D. discontinue all training

36. For a supervisor to have his cleaning employees willing to follow standardized cleaning procedures, he must be prepared to

    A. associate with his employees
    B. show that the procedures are reasonable
    C. give extra time off
    D. set up a penalty system

37. One of the employees you supervise has broken the rule against keeping liquor in his locker.
    You should

    A. make believe it never happened and forget the incident
    B. explain the rule to him and that a repetition may result in disciplinary action
    C. suspend him immediately
    D. fire him immediately

38. The BEST action for you to take on receiving complaints of poor illumination in one of the offices is to

    A. wait until you have several complaints of this kind
    B. tell the complainant nothing can be done
    C. request that additional ceiling lights be installed
    D. check the office for the cause of poor illumination

39. The MAIN purpose of periodic inspections and tests of mechanical equipment is to

    A. keep the men busy during otherwise slack periods
    B. discover minor faults before they develop into major faults
    C. make the men familiar with the equipment
    D. encourage the men to take better care of the equipment

40. Assume that one of your employees has been slightly injured while doing a cleaning job. After the employee has been cared for, you should NEXT

    A. investigate the cause of the accident
    B. notify the union
    C. charge the employee with recklessness
    D. transfer the employee

KEY (CORRECT ANSWERS)

1.	B	11.	C	21.	C	31.	C
2.	D	12.	C	22.	B	32.	B
3.	B	13.	C	23.	C	33.	A
4.	C	14.	B	24.	D	34.	B
5.	B	15.	A	25.	D	35.	C
6.	D	16.	B	26.	C	36.	B
7.	C	17.	C	27.	C	37.	B
8.	C	18.	A	28.	A	38.	D
9.	A	19.	B	29.	C	39.	B
10.	A	20.	B	30.	D	40.	A

EXAMINATION SECTION
TEST 1

DIRECTIONS: Each question or incomplete statement is followed by several suggested answers or completions. Select the one that BEST answers the question or completes the statement. *PRINT THE LETTER OF THE CORRECT ANSWER IN THE SPACE AT THE RIGHT.*

1. Linseed oil is MOST commonly used to

    A. seal wooden floors
    B. polish brass fixtures
    C. thin exterior oil base paints
    D. lubricate fan bearings

2. The APPROXIMATE number of square feet of unobstructed corridor floorspace that one cleaner can sweep in an hour is

    A. 1200 B. 2400 C. 4000 D. 6000

3. Of the following materials, the one MOST effective in dusting office furniture is a

    A. silk cloth   B. chamois
    C. soft cotton cloth   D. counter brush

4. Of the following materials, the one that should be used to produce the MOST resilient flooring is

    A. concrete   B. terrazzo
    C. ceramic tile   D. asphalt tile

5. Sweeping compound is used on concrete floors MAINLY to

    A. keep the dust down
    B. polish the floor
    C. harden the floor surface
    D. indicate which part of the floor has not been swept

6. The type of floor finish or wax that will produce an anti-slip surface on resilient floor coverings is

    A. resin-based floor finish
    B. water emulsion wax
    C. paste wax
    D. paraffin

7. High sheen and good wearing qualities can be obtained when polishing a waxed floor by using an electric scrubbing machine equipped with

    A. nylon disks   B. soft brushes
    C. steel wool pads D. pumice wheels

8. Spalling of the surface of a marble floor may result if the floor is washed with

    A. a solution of trisodium phosphate   B. a soft soap solution
    C. a neutral liquid detergent solution D. cold water

9. When not in use, a broom should be stored

   A. resting on the floor with the handle end down
   B. resting on the floor with the bristle end down
   C. hanging by the handle from a hook
   D. lying flat on the floor

10. The one of the following items which ordinarily requires the MOST time to wash is a(n)

    A. 5 ft x 10 ft Venetian blind
    B. 4 ft fluorescent fixture
    C. incandescent fixture
    D. 5 ft x 10 ft ceramic tile floor

11. A broom that has been properly used should GENERALLY be replaced after

    A. it has been used for one month
    B. its bristles have been worn down by more than one-third of their original length
    C. it has been used for two months
    D. its bristles have been worn down by more than two-thirds of their original length

12. The floor area of a room which measures 10 ft long x 10 ft wide is _____ sq. ft.

    A. 20   B. 40   C. 100   D. 1000

13. The FIRST thing that should be checked before an oil-fired, low-pressure steam boiler is started up in the morning is the

    A. boiler water level
    B. stack temperature
    C. aquastat
    D. vaporstat

14. The MAIN reason for preheating number 6 fuel oil before allowing it to enter an oil burner is to

    A. increase its viscosity
    B. decrease its viscosity
    C. increase its heating value
    D. decrease its flash point

15. A house pump is used to

    A. drain basements that become flooded
    B. pump sewage from the basement to the sewer
    C. pump city water to a roof storage tank
    D. circulate domestic hot water

16. The device which shuts down an automatic rotary cup oil burner when the steam pressure reaches a preset high limit is a

    A. pressure gage
    B. pressurtrol
    C. safety valve
    D. low water cutoff

17. A pressure gage connected to a compressed air tank USUALLY reads in

    A. pounds
    B. pounds per square inch
    C. inches of mercury
    D. feet of water

18. The device which shuts off the oil burner when the water level in the boiler is too low is the

    A. feedwater regulator
    B. low water cutoff
    C. high water alarm
    D. programmer

19. The device which shuts down an oil burner when there is a flame failure is the

    A. stack switch
    B. thermostat
    C. manometer
    D. modutrol motor

20. The switch which is used to shut off the oil burner in case of a fire in the boiler room is located

    A. on the programmer cover
    B. near the boiler room entrance
    C. on the burner motor
    D. in the custodian's office

21. The MOST likely reason for a cold water faucet to continue to drip after its washer has been replaced is a defective

    A. handle   B. stem   C. seat   D. bib

22. In water lines, the type of valve which should always be either fully open or fully closed is the

    A. needle valve
    B. gate valve
    C. globe valve
    D. mixing valve

23. The BEST tool to use on a 1" galvanized iron pipe nipple when unscrewing the nipple from a coupling is a _____ wrench.

    A. crescent   B. stillson   C. monkey   D. spud

24. The BEST way to locate a leak in a natural gas pipe line is to

    A. hold a lighted match under the pipe and move it along the length of the pipe slowly
    B. hold a lighted match about two inches above the pipe and move it along the length of the pipe slowly
    C. coat the pipe with a soapy solution and watch for bubbles
    D. shut off the gas at the meter and then coat the pipe with a soapy solution and watch for bubbles

25. When comparing a 60 watt yellow bulb with a 60 watt clear bulb, it can be said that they BOTH

    A. give the same amount of light
    B. use the same amount of power
    C. will burn for at least 60 hours
    D. will burn for at least 60 days

26. The output capacity of an electric motor is USUALLY rated in   26.____

   A. kilowatts   B. horsepower
   C. percent   D. cubic feet

27. A fuse will burn out whenever it is subjected to excessive   27.____

   A. resistance   B. voltage
   C. current   D. capacitance

28. Of the following, the device which uses the GREATEST amount of electric power is the   28.____

   A. electric typewriter
   B. $\frac{1}{4}$ inch electric drill
   C. floor scrubbing machine
   D. oil burner ignition transformer

29. Meters which indicate the electric power consumed in a public building are read in   29.____

   A. kilowatt-hours B. volts
   C. cubic feet   D. degree days

30. Tongue and groove lumber is used for   30.____

   A. desk drawers   B. hardwood floors
   C. picture frames D. cabinet doors

31. When hand sawing a 1" x 4" board parallel to the grain of the wood, the BEST saw to use is the _____ saw.   31.____

   A. cross-cut   B. back
   C. hack   D. rip

32. The BEST tool to use to make a recess for the head of a flat-head wood screw is a(n)   32.____

   A. counterbore   B. countersink
   C. auger   D. nail set

33. In attaching two pieces of wood with a nut and bolt, the holes drilled should be   33.____

   A. slightly undersize in one piece, slightly oversize in the other
   B. slightly oversize in both pieces
   C. slightly undersize in both pieces
   D. drilled from opposite sides of the joint

34. The one of the following transmission devices which should be oiled MOST often is the   34.____

   A. V-belt   B. roller chain
   C. rigid coupling D. clutch plate

35. A motor-generator set is USUALLY part of a(n)   35.____

   A. steam boiler   B. hydraulic elevator
   C. electric elevator D. incinerator

36. The one of the following devices which MOST frequently contains hydraulic fluid is a   36.____

   A. door closer
   B. worm gear reducer
   C. foam fire extinguisher
   D. hand winch

37. A breakdown of the causes of accidental injuries by percent would show that such injuries are *most nearly* caused   37.____

   A. 100 percent by unsafe physical working conditions
   B. 100 percent by unsafe acts of people
   C. 50 percent by unsafe physical working conditions and 50 percent by unsafe acts of people
   D. 20 percent by unsafe physical working conditions and 80 percent by unsafe acts of people

38. When using an eight-foot stepladder, a worker should climb up not more than _____ rungs.   38.____

   A. 4   B. 5   C. 6   D. 7

39. A supervisor interested in the safety of his subordinates would NOT permit   39.____

   A. using a wooden rule to take measurements near electrical apparatus
   B. using a machinist's hammer to strike a chisel
   C. removing metal chips from a machine with a rag
   D. testing the heat of a soldering iron with a piece of solder

40. If a worker feels an electric shock while using a portable electric drill, he should immediately   40.____

   A. stand on a piece of scrap lumber
   B. reverse the plug in the receptacle
   C. hold onto a grounded pipe or piece of metal
   D. take the drill out of service

KEY (CORRECT ANSWERS)

1.	C	11.	B	21.	C	31.	D
2.	D	12.	C	22.	B	32.	B
3.	C	13.	A	23.	B	33.	B
4.	D	14.	A	24.	C	34.	B
5.	A	15.	C	25.	B	35.	C
6.	A	16.	B	26.	B	36.	A
7.	B	17.	B	27.	C	37.	D
8.	A	18.	B	28.	C	38.	C
9.	C	19.	A	29.	A	39.	C
10.	A	20.	B	30.	B	40.	D

TEST 2

DIRECTIONS: Each question or incomplete statement is followed by several suggested answers or completions. Select the one that BEST answers the question or completes the statement. *PRINT THE LETTER OF THE CORRECT ANSWER IN THE SPACE AT THE RIGHT.*

1. During a shortage of custodial help in a public building, the cleaning task which will probably receive LEAST attention is   1.____

    A. picking up sweepings
    B. emptying ashtrays
    C. washing walls
    D. dust-mopping offices

2. Of the following substances commonly used on floors, the MOST flammable is   2.____

    A. resin-based floor finish
    B. floor sealer
    C. water emulsion wax
    D. trisodium phosphate

3. The MOST effective method for cleaning badly soiled carpeting is   3.____

    A. wet shampooing
    B. vacuum cleaning
    C. dry shampooing
    D. wire brushing

4. Before repainting becomes necessary, a painted wall can USUALLY be washed completely   4.____

    A. only once
    B. two or three times
    C. eight to ten times
    D. sixteen to twenty times

5. The FIRST step in routine cleaning of offices at night should be   5.____

    A. sweeping floors
    B. emptying ashtrays
    C. dusting furniture
    D. damp mopping the floors

6. Among the factors pertaining to the maintenance and cleaning of a building, the one MOST likely to be under the control of the building custodian is the   6.____

    A. size of the area
    B. density of occupancy
    C. type of occupancy
    D. standards to be maintained

7. "Treated" or "dustless" sweeping of resilient-type floors requires   7.____

    A. spraying the floors with water to keep the dust down
    B. spreading sweeping compound on the floor
    C. sweeping cloths that are chemically treated with mineral oil
    D. spraying the sweeping tool with neatsfoot oil

8. A modern central vacuum cleaner system   8.____

    A. is cheaper to operate than one portable machine
    B. generally produces less suction than a portable machine
    C. conveys the dirt directly to a basement tank
    D. must be operated only in the daytime

9. Oxalic acid can be used to

   A. remove ink spots from wood
   B. clear floor drains
   C. solder copper flashing
   D. polish brass

10. The BEST material for sealing a terrazzo floor is

    A. varnish
    B. a penetrating seal
    C. shellac
    D. a surface seal

11. The MOST troublesome feature in cleaning public washrooms is

    A. cleaning and deodorizing the urinals
    B. washing the toilet bowls
    C. mopping the tile floors
    D. removing chewing gum from the floors

12. In order to improve its appearance, extend its life, and reduce the labor involved in dusting, wood furniture should be polished with

    A. an oil polish
    B. a water emulsion wax
    C. a silicone and spirit chemical spray
    D. clear water

13. Ringelmann charts are useful in determining

    A. interest rates
    B. smoke density
    C. standard times for cleaning operations
    D. fuel consumption

14. A fusible plug is USUALLY found in a

    A. lighting panel
    B. fire door
    C. boiler wall
    D. house tank

15. In an air conditioned office, MOST people would feel comfortable when the room temperature and humidity are maintained, respectively, at

    A. 75° F and 50%
    B. 70° F and 30%
    C. 75° F and 20%
    D. 65° F and 75%

16. The one of the following sets of conditions which will provide the MOST efficient combustion in an oil-fired low-temperature steam boiler is _____ stack temperature, _____ CO_2.

    A. 400° F, 12%
    B. 500° F, 10%
    C. 600° F, 8%
    D. 700° F, 6%

17. The BEST way for a building custodian to tell if the night cleaners have done their work well is to check

    A. on how much cleaning material has been used
    B. on how much waste paper was collected
    C. the building for cleanliness
    D. the floor mops to see if they are still wet

18. The one of the following which is the BEST reason for introducing a training program is that the

    A. quality of work is above standard
    B. employees are all experienced
    C. accident rate is too high
    D. tenant complaints are negligible

19. The FIRST step in training an inexperienced individual in a particular job is to

    A. put him to work and watch for mistakes
    B. put him to work and tell him to call for help if he needs it
    C. put him at ease and then find out what he knows about the work
    D. tell him to watch the least experienced worker on the job because the training is still fresh in his mind

20. As used in job analysis, the term "job breakdown" means

    A. any equipment failure
    B. any failure on the part of the worker to complete the job
    C. dividing the job into a series of steps
    D. reducing the number of workers by 50 percent

21. At times when a public building is closed to the public, the building custodian should

    A. keep all doors locked and admit no one
    B. admit only custodial employees
    C. admit anyone as long as he signs the log
    D. admit only those who have business in the building

22. When a public building is equipped for security purposes with exterior lights on or around the building, the lights should be kept lit

    A. all night except for Saturdays, Sundays, and holidays
    B. twenty-four hours a day on weekends
    C. throughout the night, every night of the week
    D. until midnight, every night of the week

23. Custodial workers are MOST liable to injury when they are engaged in

    A. sweeping floors   B. mopping floors
    C. dusting furniture   D. moving furniture

24. The BEST place to store a wooden stepladder is 24._____

    A. in a boiler room
    B. in a stairwell
    C. in a dry room
    D. outside a basement window provided that there is a locked grating overhead

25. Of the following, the BEST action for a building custodian to take when he notices that an office worker in his building has a hot plate connected to a heavily loaded electric circuit is to 25._____

    A. remove the hot plate from the office when its owner is not present
    B. demand that the office worker remove the hot plate immediately
    C. write a report to the supervisor of the office requesting corrective action
    D. ignore the situation

26. In dealing with the public, a building custodian should be 26._____

    A. indulgent   B. courteous
    C. disagreeable   D. unavailable

27. If a building custodian sees a group of people in front of his building preparing to form a picket line, he should 27._____

    A. turn on a lawn sprinkler to spray the pickets
    B. order the pickets off the sidewalk in front of the building
    C. show the pickets he is sympathetic with their complaint
    D. contact his supervisor immediately for instructions

28. When electric service in a public building is to be shut off from 10 A.M. Tuesday to 11:30 the next morning because a new electric feeder cable is being installed, the building custodian should 28._____

    A. prepare a memo to all office supervisors in the building, notifying them of the situation, and deliver a copy to each office as soon as possible
    B. prepare a notice of the impending power stoppage and post it in the lobby early Tuesday morning
    C. tell the electrical contractor to notify the tenants when he is about to shut off the power
    D. discontinue elevator service at 10 A.M. on Tuesday as an indication to the tenants that the power supply is off

29. The BEST way to remove some small pieces of broken glass from a floor is to 29._____

    A. use a brush and dustpan
    B. pick up the pieces carefully with your hands
    C. use a wet mop and a wringer
    D. sweep the pieces into the corner of the room

30. There is a two-light fixture in the room where you are working. One of the light bulbs goes out, and you need more light to work by. You should 30._____

    A. change the fuse in the fuse box
    B. have a new bulb put in
    C. call for an electrician and stop work till he comes
    D. find out what is causing the short circuit

31. While working on the job, you accidently break a window pane. No one is around, and you are able to clean up the broken pieces of glass. It would then be BEST for you to

   A. leave a note near the window that a new glass has to be put in because it was accidently broken
   B. forget about the whole thing because the window was not broken on purpose
   C. write a report to your supervisor telling him that you saw a broken window pane that has to be fixed
   D. tell your supervisor that you accidently broke the window pane while working

32. Many machines have certain safety devices for the operators. The MOST important reason for having these safety devices is to

   A. increase the amount of work that the machines can do
   B. permit repairs to be made on the machines without shutting them down
   C. help prevent accidents to people who use the machines
   D. reduce the cost of electric power needed to run the machines

Questions 33-36.

DIRECTIONS: Answer Questions 33 through 36 only according to the information given in the following passage.

MOPPING FLOORS

When mopping hardened cement floors, either painted or unpainted, a soap and water mixture should be used. This should be made by dissolving 1/2 a cup of soft soap in a pail of hot water. It is not desirable, however, under any circumstances, to use a soap and water mixture on cement floors that are not hardened. For mopping this type of floor, it is recommended that the cleaning agent be made up of 2 ounces of laundry soda mixed in a pail of water.

Soaps are not generally used on hard tile floors because slippery films may build up on the floor. It is generally recommended that these floors be mopped using a pail of hot water in which has been mixed 2 ounces of washing powder for each gallon of water. The floors should then be rinsed thoroughly.

After the mopping is finished, proper care should be taken of the mop. This is done by first cleaning the mop in clear warm water. Then it should be wrung out, after which the strands of the mop should be untangled. Finally, the mop should be hung by its handle to dry.

33. According to the above passage, you should NEVER use a soap and water mixture when mopping _____ floors.

   A. hardened cement   B. painted
   C. unhardened cement   D. unpainted

34. According to the above passage, using laundry soda mixed in a pail of water as a cleaning agent is recommended for

   A. all floors
   B. all floors except hard tile floors
   C. some cement floors
   D. linoleum floor coverings only

35. According to the above passage, the GENERALLY recommended mixture for mopping hard tile floors is

   A. 1/2 cup of soft soap for each gallon of hot water
   B. 1/2 cup of soft soap in a pail of hot water
   C. 2 ounces of washing powder in a pail of hot water
   D. 2 ounches of washing powder for each gallon of hot water

36. According to the above passage, the PROPER care of a mop after it is used includes

   A. cleaning it in clear cold water and hanging it by its handle to dry
   B. wringing it out, untangling, and drying it
   C. untangling its strands before wringing it out
   D. untangling its strands while cleaning it in clear water

Questions 37-40.

DIRECTIONS: Answer Questions 37 through 40 only according to the information given in the following passage.

ACCIDENT PREVENTION

Many accidents and injuries can be prevented if employees learn to be move careful. The wearing of shoes with thin or badly worn soles or open toes can easily lead to foot injuries from tacks, nails, and chair and desk legs. Loose or torn clothing should not be worn near moving machinery. This is especially true of neckties which can very easily become caught in the machine. You should not place objects so that they block or partly block hallways, corridors, or other passageways. Even when they are stored in the proper place, tools, supplies, and equipment should be carefully placed or piled so as not to fall, nor have anything stick out from a pile. Before cabinets, lockers or ladders are moved, the tops should be cleared of anything which might injure someone or fall off. If necessary, use a dolly to move these or other bulky objects.

Despite all efforts to avoid accidents and injuries, however, some will happen. If an employee is injured, no matter how small the injury, he should report it to his supervisor and have the injury treated. A small cut that is not attended to can easily become infected and can cause more trouble than some injuries which at first seem more serious. It never pays to take chances.

37. According to the above passage, the one statement that is NOT true is that

   A. by being more careful, employees can reduce the number of accidents that happen
   B. women should wear shoes with open toes for comfort when working
   C. supplies should be piled so that nothing is sticking out from the pile
   D. if an employee sprains his wrist at work, he should tell his supervisor about it

38. According to the above passage, you should NOT wear loose clothing when you are

   A. in a corridor   B. storing tools
   C. opening cabinets   D. near moving machinery

39. According to the above passage, before moving a ladder, you should

   A. test all the rungs
   B. get a dolly to carry the ladder at all times
   C. remove everything from the top of the ladder which might fall off
   D. remove your necktie

40. According to the above passage, an employee who gets a slight cut should

   A. have it treated to help prevent infection
   B. know that a slight cut becomes more easily infected than a big cut
   C. pay no attention to it as it can't become serious
   D. realize that it is more serious than any other type of injury

KEY (CORRECT ANSWERS)

1. C	11. A	21. D	31. D
2. B	12. C	22. C	32. C
3. A	13. B	23. D	33. C
4. B	14. C	24. C	34. C
5. B	15. A	25. C	35. D
6. D	16. A	26. B	36. B
7. C	17. C	27. D	37. B
8. C	18. C	28. A	38. D
9. A	19. C	29. A	39. C
10. B	20. C	30. B	40. A

TEST 3

DIRECTIONS: Each question or incomplete statement is followed by several suggested answers or completions. Select the one that BEST answers the question or completes the statement. *PRINT THE LETTER OF THE CORRECT ANSWER IN THE SPACE AT THE RIGHT.*

1. An electric motor fire should be put out with an extinguisher that uses 1.____

    A. carbon dioxide
    B. soda-acid
    C. foam
    D. a pump tank

2. The charge in a soda-acid fire extinguisher should be replaced once 2.____

    A. a month
    B. every three months
    C. every six months
    D. a year

3. An elevator machinery room should have a fire extinguisher of the _____ type. 3.____

    A. soda-acid
    B. foam
    C. carbon dioxide
    D. sand pail

4. The national flag should be raised 4.____

    A. slowly and lowered briskly
    B. briskly and lowered slowly
    C. briskly and lowered briskly
    D. slowly and lowered slowly

5. The material which is used to seal the outside edges of a pane of window glass is 5.____

    A. stellite
    B. putty
    C. plastic wood
    D. caulking compound

6. The ceiling of a room which measures 20 ft x 30 ft is to be given two coats of paint. If one gallon of paint will cover 500 square feet, the two coats of paint will require a MINIMUM of _____ gallons. 6.____

    A. 1.5   B. 2   C. 2.4   D. 3.2

7. Rubbish, sticks, and papers on the lawn in front of a building should be collected by using a 7.____

    A. rake
    B. broom
    C. paper sticker
    D. hoe

8. Mortar stains on brickwork can be scrubbed off by using a solution of 8.____

    A. benzine
    B. tri-sodium phosphate
    C. muriatic acid
    D. acetic acid

9. The BEST chemical for melting ice on sidewalks is 9.____

    A. sodium chloride
    B. calcium carbonate
    C. hydrogen sulphide
    D. calcium chloride

10. Before painting a kitchen wall,
    A. a degreaser must be mixed with the paint
    B. all traces of grease must be washed off
    C. a water-base paint must be used to dissolve the grease
    D. the walls must be sanded to remove all traces of grease and old paint

11. For interior walls which must be washed very often, the PREFERRED paint is
    A. enamel   B. flat
    C. exterior varnish   D. calsomine

12. A type of window which is USUALLY equipped with sash cords or chains is the _____ type.
    A. hopper   B. awning
    C. casement   D. double-hung

13. The slats of a Venetian blind are usually tilted by a device containing a _____ gear.
    A. worm   B. spur   C. hypoid   D. bevil

14. When washing the outside of a window with a narrow inside sill, a window cleaner should place his water pail on
    A. the outside window sill
    B. the nearest desk or chair
    C. a radiator at the center of the window
    D. the floor at a convenient point toward one side of the window

15. In order to determine the carrying capacity of a passenger elevator, a custodian would have to
    A. measure the floor area
    B. check the diameter of the cable
    C. read the inspection certificate
    D. read the motor nameplate

16. Before pruning a tree, the FIRST step should be to determine
    A. if there is insect infestation
    B. the general health of the tree
    C. the desired results
    D. amount of excess foliage

17. Tree fertilizer should have a high content of
    A. slaked lime   B. chlordane
    C. rose dust   D. nitrogen

18. A gasoline-driven snow blower should be stored for the summer with its fuel tank
    A. filled with gasoline
    B. and fuel lines drained
    C. filled with water
    D. half filled with number 4 fuel oil

19. A pipe that "sweats" in the summer time PROBABLY contains 19.____

   A. hot water
   B. low pressure steam
   C. domestic gas
   D. cold water

20. A good preventive maintenance program requires that each item of equipment be 20.____

   A. represented by an up-to-date record card on file
   B. lubricated daily
   C. brand new at the start of the program
   D. painted inside and out

Questions 21-24.

DIRECTIONS: Questions 21 through 24, inclusive, are to be answered SOLELY on the basis of the following paragraph.

All cleaning agents and supplies should be kept in a central storeroom which should be kept looked and only the custodian, storekeeper and foreman should have keys. Shelving should be provided for the smaller items, while barrels containing scouring powder or other bulk material should be set on the floor or on special cradles. Each compartment in the shelves should be marked plainly and only the item indicated stored therein. Each barrel should also be marked plainly. It may also be desirable to keep special items such as electric lamps, flashlight batteries, etc., in a locked cabinet or separate room to which only the custodian and the night building foreman have keys.

21. According to the above paragraph, scouring powder 21.____

   A. should be kept on shelves
   B. comes in one-pound cans
   C. should be kept in a locked cabinet
   D. is a bulk material

22. According to the above paragraph, 22.____

   A. the storekeeper should not be entrusted with the safekeeping of light bulbs
   B. flashlight batteries should be stored in barrels
   C. the central storeroom should be kept locked
   D. only special items should be stored under lock and key

23. According to the above paragraph, 23.____

   A. each shelf compartment should contain at least four different items
   B. barrels must be stored in cradles
   C. all items stored should be in marked compartments
   D. crates of light bulbs should be stored in cradles

24. As used in the above paragraph, the word *cradle* means a 24.____

   A. dolly
   B. support
   C. doll's bed
   D. hand truck

Questions 25-28.

DIRECTIONS: Questions 25 through 28, inclusive, are to be answered SOLELY on the basis of the following paragraph.

There are on the market many cleaning agents for which amazing claims are made. Chemical analysis shows that the majority of them are well-known chemicals slightly modified and packaged and sold under various trade names. For that reason, the agents which have been selected for your use are those whose cleaning properties are well-known and whose use can be standardized. It is obviously undesirable to offer too wide a selection as that would be confusing to the cleaner, but a sufficient number must be provided so that a satisfactory agent is available for each task.

25. According to the above paragraph,

    A. there are few cleaning agents on the market
    B. there are no really good cleaning agents on the market
    C. cleaning agents are sold under several different brand names
    D. all cleaning agents are the same

26. According to the above paragraph,

    A. all cleaning agents should be chemically analyzed before use
    B. the best cleaning agents are those for which no claims are made by the manufacturer
    C. different cleaning agents may be needed for different tasks
    D. all cleaning agents have been standardized by the federal government

27. As used in the above paragraph, the word *amazing* means

    A. illegal
    B. untrue
    C. astonishing
    D. specific

28. As used in the above paragraph, the word *modified* means

    A. changed
    B. refined
    C. labelled
    D. diluted

29. The MAIN reason for keeping an inventory of housekeeping supplies is to

    A. be sure that supplies are available when needed
    B. determine the cost of the supplies
    C. automatically prevent waste of the supplies
    D. be sure that at least two years' supplies are on hand at all times

30. Current daily records are MOST desirable in dealing with problems concerning

    A. accidents
    B. vandalism
    C. employee time and attendance
    D. the consumption of electricity

31. The continuous record of activities taking place in a boiler room is called a

    A. computer
    B. data bank
    C. log book
    D. time sheet

32. The one of the following subjects of a fire prevention training program which is MOST readily applied on the job is the

   A. elimination of fire hazards
   B. use of portable fire extinguishers
   C. knowledge of types of fires
   D. method of reporting fires

33. A good supervisor will NOT

   A. tell his men what their jobs are and why they are important
   B. show his men how their jobs are to be done in the right way
   C. require some of the men to do their jobs in the presence of the supervisor demonstrating that they understand the job
   D. leave his men alone because they will always do their jobs correctly once they have received their instructions

34. When a supervisor sees a worker doing his job incorrectly, he should

   A. tell the worker to be more careful
   B. suspend the worker until he learns to do the job correctly
   C. tell the worker specifically how the job should be done
   D. scold the man

35. An office worker complains to a custodian that one of the cleaners broke off a branch of a plant which she kept on her desk and that she can identify the cleaner.
   The BEST thing for the custodian to do is to

   A. convince her that the plant will grow another branch eventually
   B. make the cleaner apologize and pay for a new plant out of his own pocket
   C. sympathize with the office worker and assure her that he will speak to the cleaner about it
   D. tell her not to bother him about her personal property

36. An employee who is a good worker but is often late for work

   A. is lazy and should be dismissed
   B. cannot tell time
   C. can have no excuse for being late more than once a month
   D. should be questioned by his supervisor to try to find out why he is late

37. When starting any disciplinary action, a good supervisor should

   A. show his annoyance by losing his temper
   B. be apologetic
   C. be sarcastic
   D. be firm and positive

38. Good public relations can be damaged by a custodian who treats tenants, fellow workers, friends, relatives, and the public with

   A. courtesy   B. consideration
   C. contempt   D. respect

39. The BEST way for a supervisor to maintain good employee morale is to 39.____
    A. avoid praising any one employee
    B. always have an alibi for his own mistakes
    C. encourage cliques by given them information before giving it to other workers
    D. give adequate credit and praise when due

40. When a new employee reports to a custodian on his first day on the job, the custodian should 40.____
    A. extend a hearty welcome and make the new employee feel welcome
    B. have the man sit and wait for a while before seeing him so that the employee realizes how busy the custodian is
    C. warn him of stern disciplinary action if he is late or absent excessively
    D. tell him he probably will have difficulty doing the work so that he doesn't become overconfident

---

KEY (CORRECT ANSWERS)

1. A	11. A	21. D	31. C
2. D	12. D	22. C	32. A
3. C	13. A	23. C	33. D
4. B	14. D	24. B	34. C
5. B	15. C	25. C	35. C
6. C	16. C	26. C	36. D
7. A	17. D	27. C	37. D
8. C	18. B	28. A	38. C
9. D	19. D	29. A	39. D
10. B	20. A	30. C	40. A

EXAMINATION SECTION
TEST 1

DIRECTIONS: Each question or incomplete statement is followed by several suggested answers or completions. Select the one that BEST answers the question or completes the statement. *PRINT THE LETTER OF THE CORRECT ANSWER IN THE SPACE AT THE RIGHT.*

1. The pipe fitting that would be used to connect a 2" pipe at a 45° angle to another 2" pipe is called a(n)

    A. tee
    B. orifice flange
    C. reducer
    D. elbow

2. An instrument that measures relative humidity is called a(n)

    A. manometer
    B. interferemeter
    C. hygrometer
    D. petrometer

3. The one of the following flat drive-belts that gives the BEST service in dry places is a(n) _____ belt.

    A. rawhide
    B. oak-tanned
    C. chrome-tanned
    D. semirawhide

4. The letter representing the standard V-belt section which has the LOWEST horsepower-per-belt rating is

    A. E
    B. C
    C. B
    D. A

5. A 6 x 19 wire rope has

    A. 6 strands
    B. 6 wires in each strand
    C. 19 strands
    D. 25 strands arranged in a 6 x 19 pattern

6. A water tank 5 feet in diameter and 30 feet high has a volume of MOST NEARLY _____ cubic feet.

    A. 150
    B. 250
    C. 600
    D. 1200

7. The circumference of a circle with a radius of 5 inches is MOST NEARLY _____ inches.

    A. 31.3
    B. 30.0
    C. 20.1
    D. 13.4

8. A flexible coupling should be used to connect two shafts that

    A. have centerlines at right angles to each other
    B. may be slightly out of line
    C. start and stop too fast
    D. have different speeds

9. Of the following materials used to make pipe, the one that is MOST brittle is

    A. lead
    B. aluminum
    C. copper
    D. cast iron

10. Mechanical equipment is generally tested and inspected on regular schedules in order to

   A. avoid breakdowns
   B. train new personnel
   C. maintain inventory
   D. give employees something to do

11. The *united inches* for a pane of glass that measures 14 inches by 20 inches is

   A. 14   B. 34   C. 40   D. 54

12. The one of the following that should NOT be lubricated is a(n)

   A. spur gear train   B. motor commutator
   C. roller chain drive   D. automobile axle

13. One of the following oils that has the LOWEST viscosity is S.A.E.

   A. 70   B. 50   C. 20   D. 10W

14. A neoprene gasket would normally be used in a pipeline carrying

   A. steam   B. compressed air
   C. carbon dioxide   D. light oil

15. The one of the following that would NOT be used in cleaning toilet bowls is

   A. a cleaning cloth   B. oxalic acid
   C. muriatic acid   D. a detergent

16. An electric motor driven air compressor is automatically started and stopped by a

   A. thermostat   B. line air valve
   C. pressure switch   D. float trap

17. The term *kilowatt hours* describes the consumption of

   A. energy   B. radiation
   C. cooling capacity   D. conductance

18. AC voltage may be converted to DC voltage by means of a

   A. magnet   B. rectifier
   C. voltage regulator   D. transducer

19. When replacing a blown fuse, it is BEST to

   A. install another one of slightly larger size
   B. seek the cause of the fuse failure before replacing it
   C. install another one of size smaller
   D. read the electric meters as a check on the condition of the circuit

20. A 208 volt, 3 phase, 4 wire circuit power supply has a line to grounded neutral voltage of APPROXIMATELY _____ volts.

   A. 120   B. 208   C. 220   D. 240

21. An interlock is generally installed on electronic equipment to 21.____

   A. prevent loss of power
   B. maintain VHF frequencies
   C. keep the vacuum tubes lit
   D. prevent electric shock during maintenance operations

22. A flame should not be used to inspect the electrolyte level in a lead-acid battery because 22.____
    the battery cells give off highly flammable

   A. hydrogen   B. lead oxide
   C. lithium   D. xenon

23. The purpose of the third prong in a three-prong male electric plug used in a 120 volt circuit is to 23.____

   A. make a firm connection   B. strengthen the plug
   C. ground to prevent shock   D. act as a transducer

24. A school custodian engineer on duty is informed that an employee under his supervision 24.____
    has just been injured in the school building.
    The FIRST course of action he should take is to

   A. inform his superior
   B. aid the injured employee
   C. call a meeting of all the men
   D. order an investigation

25. In the prevention of accidental injuries, the MOST effective procedure is to 25.____

   A. install safety guards
   B. alert the workers to the hazards
   C. install lighting for easy sight
   D. eliminate the accident hazard

KEY (CORRECT ANSWERS)

1. D
2. C
3. B
4. D
5. A

6. C
7. A
8. B
9. D
10. A

11. B
12. B
13. D
14. D
15. C

16. C
17. A
18. B
19. B
20. A

21. D
22. A
23. C
24. B
25. D

TEST 2

DIRECTIONS: Each question or incomplete statement is followed by several suggested answers or completions. Select the one that BEST answers the question or completes the statement. *PRINT THE LETTER OF THE CORRECT ANSWER IN THE SPACE AT THE RIGHT.*

1. The one of the following practices that will INCREASE the possibility of school fires occurring is the

    A. using of understairs areas for storage of all kinds
    B. wiping of machinery shafts with lubricating oil
    C. ventilating of all storage spaces
    D. cleaning of lockers at frequent intervals

    1.____

2. When evaluating a building for fire hazards, the MOST important considerations are the

    A. number of stories and the height of each story
    B. location in the neighborhood and the accessibility
    C. interior lighting and the furniture
    D. number of residents and the use of the building

    2.____

3. The one of the following that is a basic safety requirement for operating a power mower is:

    A. Fill gasoline driven mower indoors
    B. Do not operate power mowers on wet grass
    C. Keep the motor running when you leave the mower unattended for only a short while
    D. Fill the tank while the engine is running

    3.____

4. You observe a red truck making a fuel delivery to your school.
   The fuel being delivered is PROBABLY

    A. gasoline   B. #2 fuel oil
    C. #4 fuel oil   D. #5 fuel oil

    4.____

5. The one of the following steps that is NOT taken when operating a carbon dioxide fire extinguisher is to

    A. carry the extinguisher to the fire and set it on the ground
    B. unhook the hose
    C. pull the pin in the valve wheel
    D. turn the valve and direct the gas to the top of the fire

    5.____

6. The BEST course of action to take to settle a job-related dispute that has arisen among two of your employees is to

    A. bring them both together, listen to their arguments, and then make a decision
    B. tell the two employees individually to settle their dispute
    C. tell both employees to submit their dispute in writing to you and then make a decision
    D. listen to the argument of each one separately and then make a decision

    6.____

7. A school custodian engineer accidentally discovers a bottle of whiskey in a staff member's desk.
   The BEST procedure for the custodian to follow is to

   A. verbally reprimand him and prefer departmental charges
   B. inform him that whiskey is not allowed in school buildings
   C. call a meeting of all the employees and tell them what you found
   D. do nothing, as you do not want to embarrass the person

8. A new employee under your supervision constantly reports late for work.
   The one of the following actions you should take FIRST is to

   A. admonish him in front of the other employees
   B. prefer charges against him
   C. transfer him to another school
   D. warn him that he must be on time

9. The one of the following procedures that is BEST to follow when it is necessary to reprimand a worker is to

   A. issue the same reprimand to all of your men
   B. avoid him so he won't feel bad
   C. speak to him privately about the matter
   D. tell him what he has done wrong immediately to teach the other employees a lesson

10. The LEAST important factor to consider when evaluating the work of an employee is

    A. his grade on his civil service test
    B. the quality of his work
    C. his resourcefulness
    D. his attendance record

11. The one of the following supervisory actions that a school custodian engineer should use LEAST often is:

    A. Make periodic reports to his superior about the work of his men
    B. Bring employees up on *charges* whenever they do anything wrong
    C. Listen to staff grievances
    D. Advise an employee concerning a personal problem

12. The MAIN supervisory responsibility of a school custodian engineer is to

    A. foster policies of the Board of Education and the parents' organizations
    B. do his job so well that the students and employees like him
    C. make assignments to his employees
    D. operate and maintain facilities in a safe and efficient manner

13. One of your employees verbally protests to you about your evaluation of his work.
    The BEST way to handle him is to

    A. advise him of your lengthy and qualified experience
    B. tell him that you do not care to talk about it
    C. explain to him how you arrived at your evaluation

D. tell him that since all of the other employees are satisfied, he should withdraw his complaint

14. A school custodian engineer will BEST keep the morales of his men high by

    A. giving praise for well-done work
    B. assigning good workers the most work
    C. personally helping each man in all the details of the man's job
    D. allowing special privileges for good work

15. In training maintenance personnel under the supervision of a school custodian engineer, the one of the following that should be given LEAST consideration by the custodian is

    A. how the training is to be given
    B. who is to be trained
    C. when the training will be given
    D. how the school principal wants them to be trained

16. The BEST attitude for a school custodian engineer to follow in his dealings with the public is to

    A. offer aid and cooperation to the public whenever possible
    B. show authority so that the public knows the limits to which they may make requests
    C. ignore the public, since the custodian has a specific job to do
    D. refer the public to a higher authority for solution of all their problems

17. The students playing in the schoolyard consistently lose rubber balls that land on the school roof. They request that you, the school custodian engineer, retrieve these balls.
    Of the following, the BEST procedure for you to follow is:

    A. Teach them a lesson and refuse to retrieve the balls
    B. Retrieve the balls and throw them into the incinerator
    C. One day a week retrieve the balls and return them to the students
    D. Retrieve the balls and give them to a local children's charity

18. The president of a charitable organization requests a permit to use the school building. You, the school custodian engineer, note that his same organization used the school previously and did not observe the *NO SMOKING* rules.
    The BEST procedure for you to follow is to

    A. deny the organization a permit since they did not obey the school regulations before
    B. issue the permit without any questions since a large group is difficult to control
    C. inform the president that if any of his members continue to disregard the no smoking rules, future permits will not be issued
    D. inform the president that if any of his members continue to disregard the no smoking rules, you will evict them from the school building

19. Due to some grievances, parents occupy your school on a weekend and refuse to leave. As the school principal is out of town and unavailable, the BEST procedure for you, the school custodian engineer on duty, is to

    A. tell your employees to vacate the school
    B. call the police department

C. cooperate with the parents on the takeover
D. lock all the people in the school

20. An organization requests a permit to use the school auditorium from the hours of 7 PM to 10 PM on a Tuesday evening. The organization also requests that its members be allowed to enter the school earlier than 7 PM and leave later than 10 PM.
The BEST procedure for you, the school custodian engineer, to follow is to

   A. inform the organization leader that the organization may only use the school from the hours of 7 PM to
   B. 10 PM
   C. issue the permit without saying anything as you want to maintain good public relations
   D. refer the matter to the school principal as you do not want to get involved
   E. ask the organization leader the reasons for the request and if the request is fair, issue the permit and let the organization do as it pleases

21. Dog owners in the neighborhood have been disregarding the *Curb Your Dog* signs and walking their dogs on your school lawn. You find that this interferes with the operation of powered lawn mowing equipment.
Your BEST procedure to follow is to

   A. put up a higher fence
   B. chase the people and dogs away
   C. tell the owners you will call the police department
   D. explain the problem to the owners and ask them to curb their dogs

22. A cleaner reports to the school custodian engineer that a particular school room is consistently messy and dirty.
The one who is equally at fault as the students for this dirty room is the

   A. students' parents
   B. regular classroom teacher
   C. student peer group
   D. cleaner for reporting the matter

23. A parent walks into a school custodian's office and starts to shout at him about a claimed injustice to her child. The PROPER procedure for the school custodian to follow is:

   A. Call the police department
   B. Summon the security guards
   C. Vacate the office
   D. Escort the parent to a guidance counselor

24. A newspaper reporter visiting a school should NORMALLY be referred to the

   A. school principal
   B. school custodian
   C. assistant superintendent of schools
   D. borough supervisor of school custodians

25. The parents of children in the neighborhood of your school complain to you that their children cannot use the school playground after school hours because the gates are closed. The BEST procedure for you to follow is to
    A. tell the parents the gates will remain closed after school hours
    B. arrange for the children to use a play street
    C. tell the parents to meet with the Board of Education on this matter
    D. try to arrange for the school gates to be open to a later hour after school hours

---

KEY (CORRECT ANSWERS)

1. A
2. D
3. B
4. A
5. D

6. A
7. B
8. D
9. C
10. A

11. B
12. D
13. C
14. A
15. D

16. A
17. C
18. C
19. B
20. A

21. D
22. B
23. D
24. A
25. D

EXAMINATION SECTION
TEST 1

DIRECTIONS: Each question or incomplete statement is followed by several suggested answers or completions. Select the one that BEST answers the question or completes the statement. *PRINT THE LETTER OF THE CORRECT ANSWER IN THE SPACE AT THE RIGHT.*

1. Of the following daily jobs in the schedule of a custodian, the one he should do FIRST in the morning is to

    A. hang out the flag
    B. open all doors of the school
    C. fire boilers
    D. dust principal's office

    1._____

2. When a school custodian is newly assigned to a building at the start of the school term, his FIRST step should be to

    A. examine the building to determine needed maintenance and repair
    B. meet the principal and discuss plans for operation and maintenance of the building
    C. call a meeting of the teaching and custodial staff to explain his plans for the building
    D. review the records of maintenance and operation left by the previous custodian

    2._____

3. A detergent is a material used GENERALLY for

    A. coating floors to resist water
    B. snow removal
    C. insulation of steam and hot water lines
    D. cleaning purposes

    3._____

4. A good disinfectant is one that will

    A. have a clean odor which will cover up disagreeable odors
    B. destroy germs and create more sanitary conditions
    C. dissolve encrusted dirt and other sources of disagreeable odors
    D. dissolve grease and other materials that may cause stoppages in toilet waste lines

    4._____

5. To help prevent leaks at the joints of water lines, the pipe threads are commonly covered with

    A. tar
    B. cup grease
    C. rubber cement
    D. white lead

    5._____

6. The advantage of using screws instead of nails is:

    A. They have greater holding power
    B. They are available in a greater variety than are nails
    C. A hammer is not required for joining wood members
    D. They are less expensive

    6._____

7. Of the following, the grade of steel wool that is FINEST is

    A. 00   B. 0   C. 1   D. 2

    7._____

8. The material used with solder to make it stick better is   8._____

   A. oakum   B. lye   C. oil   D. flux

9. In using a floor brush in a corridor, a cleaner should be instructed to   9._____

   A. use moderately long pull strokes whenever possible
   B. make certain that there is no overlap on sweeping strokes
   C. give the brush a slight jerk after each stroke to free it of loose dirt
   D. keep the sweeping surface of the brush firmly flat on the floor to obtain maximum coverage

10. Of the following, the BEST procedure in sweeping class-room floors is: 10._____

    A. Open all windows before beginning the sweeping operation
    B. The cleaner should move forward while sweeping
    C. Alternate pull and push strokes should be used
    D. Sweep under desks on both sides of an aisle while moving down the aisle

11. PROPER care of floor brushes includes   11._____

    A. washing brushes daily after each use with warm soap solution
    B. dipping brushes in kerosene periodically to remove dirt
    C. washing with warm soap solution at least once a month
    D. avoiding contact with soap or soda solutions to prevent drying of bristles

12. An advantage of vacuum cleaning rather than sweeping a floor with a floor brush is: 12._____

    A. Stationary furniture will not be touched by the cleaning tool
    B. The problem of dust on furniture is reduced
    C. The initial cost of the apparatus is less than the cost of an equivalent number of floor brushes
    D. Daily sweeping of rooms and corridors can be eliminated

13. Sweeping compound for use on rubber tiles, asphalt tile, or sealed wood floors must NOT contain   13._____

    A. sawdust   B. water   C. oil soap   D. floor oil

14. Of the following, the MOST desirable material to use in dusting furniture is a   14._____

    A. soft cotton cloth   B. hand towel
    C. counter brush   D. feather duster

15. In high dusting of walls and ceilings, the CORRECT procedure is to   15._____

    A. begin with the lower walls and proceed up to the ceiling
    B. remove pictures and window shades only if they are dusty
    C. clean the windows thoroughly before dusting any other part of the room
    D. begin with the ceiling, then dust the walls

16. When cleaning a classroom, the cleaner should   16._____

    A. dust desks before sweeping
    B. dust desks after sweeping

C. open windows wide during the desk dusting process
D. begin dusting at rows most distant from entrance door

17. Too much water on asphalt tile is objectionable MAINLY because the tile   17._____

    A. will tend to become discolored or spotted
    B. may be loosened from the floor
    C. will be softened and made uneven
    D. colors will tend to run

18. To reduce the slip hazard resulting from waxing linoleum, the MOST practical of the fol-   18._____
    lowing methods is to

    A. apply the wax in one heavy coat
    B. apply the wax after varnishing the linoleum
    C. buff the wax surface thoroughly
    D. apply the wax in several thin coats

19. Assume that the water emulsion wax needed for routine waxing in your building is 15 gal-   19._____
    lons per month. This wax is supplied in 55-gallon drums.
    To cover your needs for a year, the MINIMUM number of drums you would have to
    request is

    A. two   B. three   C. four   D. six

20. In washing down the walls, the correct procedure is to start at the bottom of the wall and   20._____
    work to the top.
    The MOST important reason for this is:

    A. Dirt streaking will tend to be avoided or easily removed
    B. Less cleansing agent will be required
    C. Rinse water will not be required
    D. The time for cleaning the wall is less than if washing started at the top of the wall

21. In mopping a wood floor of a classroom, the cleaner should   21._____

    A. mop against the grain of the wood wherever possible
    B. mop as large an area as possible at one time
    C. wet the floor before mopping with a cleaning agent
    D. mop only aisles and clear areas and use a scrub brush under desks and chairs

22. A precaution to observe in mopping asphalt tile floors is: 22._____

    A. Keep all pails off such floors because they will leave water marks
    B. Do not wear rubber footwear while mopping these floors
    C. Use circular motion in rinsing and drying the floor to avoid streaking
    D. Never use a cleaning agent containing trisodium phosphate

23. The MOST commonly used cleansing agent for the removal of ink stains from a wood   23._____
    floor is

    A. kerosene   B. oxalic acid
    C. lye   D. bicarbonate of soda

24. The FIRST operation in routine cleaning of toilets and wash rooms is to

   A. wash floors
   B. clean walls
   C. clean wash basins
   D. empty waste receptacles

25. To eliminate the cause of odors in toilet rooms, the tile floor should be mopped with

   A. a mild solution of soap and trisodium phosphate in water
   B. dilute lye solution followed by a hot water rinse
   C. dilute muriatic acid dissolved in hot water
   D. carbon tetrachloride dissolved in hot water

KEY (CORRECT ANSWERS)

1.	C	11.	C
2.	B	12.	B
3.	D	13.	D
4.	B	14.	A
5.	D	15.	D
6.	A	16.	B
7.	A	17.	B
8.	D	18.	D
9.	C	19.	C
10.	A	20.	A

21. C
22. A
23. B
24. D
25. A

TEST 2

DIRECTIONS: Each question or incomplete statement is followed by several suggested answers or completions. Select the one that BEST answers the question or completes the statement. *PRINT THE LETTER OF THE CORRECT ANSWER IN THE SPACE AT THE RIGHT.*

1. The principal reason why soap should NOT be used in cleaning windows is: 1.____

    A. It causes loosening of the putty
    B. It may cause rotting of the wood frames
    C. A film is left on the window, requiring additional rinsing
    D. Frequent use of soap will cause the glass to become permanently clouded

2. The CHIEF value of having windows consisting of many small panes of glass is 2.____

    A. the window is much stronger
    B. accident hazards are eliminated
    C. cost of replacing broken panes is low
    D. cleaning windows consisting of small panes is easier than cleaning a window with a large undivided pane

3. Cleansing powders such as Ajax should NOT be used to clean and polish brass MAINLY because 3.____

    A. the brass turns a much darker color
    B. such cleaners have no effect on tarnish
    C. the surface of the brass may become scratched
    D. too much fine dust is raised in the polishing process

4. To remove chalk marks on sidewalks and cemented playground areas, the MOST acceptable cleaning method is: 4.____

    A. Using a brush with warm water
    B. Using a brush with warm water containing some kerosene
    C. Hosing down such areas with water
    D. Using a brush with a solution of muriatic acid in water

5. The MOST important reason for oiling wood floors is that 5.____

    A. it keeps the dust from raising during the sweeping process
    B. the need for daily sweeping of classroom floors is eliminated
    C. oiled floors present a better appearance than waxed floors
    D. the wood surface will become waterproof and stain-proof

6. After oil has been sprayed on a wood floor, the sprayer should be cleaned before storing. The usual cleaning material for this purpose is 6.____

    A. ammonia water   B. salt   C. kerosene   D. alcohol

7. The MOST desirable agent for routine cleaning of slate blackboards is 7.____

    A. warm water containing trisodium phosphate
    B. mild soap solution in warm water
    C. kerosene in warm water
    D. warm water alone

8. Neatsfoot oil is COMMONLY used to

   A. oil light machinery
   B. prepare sweeping compound
   C. clean metal fixtures
   D. treat covered leather chairs

Questions 9-12.

DIRECTIONS: Column I lists cleaning agents used by a custodian. Cleaning operations are given in Column II. Select the MOST common cleaning operation for the cleaning agents listed in Column I and print the letter representing your choice in the space at the right.

COLUMN I

9. Ammonia
10. Muriatic acid
11. Carbon tetrachloride
12. Trisodium phosphate

COLUMN II

A. Add water to clean marble walls
B. Remove chewing gum from wood floors
C. Wash down calcimined ceilings
D. Add to water for washing rubber tile
E. Remove stains from porcelain

13. In order to stop a faucet from dripping, the custodian would USUALLY have to replace the

   A. cap nut   B. seat   C. washer   D. spindle

14. Drinking fountains should be adjusted so that the height of the water stream is about

   A. six inches   B. three inches
   C. one inch   D. one foot

15. Before starting up the boilers each morning, the custodian or fireman should make certain

   A. all blow-off cocks and valves are open
   B. the water is at a safe level
   C. radiator and univent valves are open
   D. the main smoke damper is fully closed

16. If the radiator on a one-pipe heating system rattles or makes noise, the PROBABLE cause is

   A. steam pressure is too high
   B. steam pressure is too low
   C. steam valve is side open
   D. radiator is air bound

17. Of the following, the LARGEST size of hard coal is

   A. chestnut   B. egg   C. stove   D. pea

18. The MAIN purpose of baffle plates in a furnace is to

   A. change the direction of flow of heated gases
   B. retard the burning of gases
   C. increase combustion rate of the fuel
   D. prevent escape of flue gases through furnace openings

19. The MAIN difference between a steam header and a steam riser for a given heating system is that the

   A. riser is usually higher than the header
   B. header is larger than the riser
   C. riser is a horizontal line and the header is a vertical line
   D. header is insulated while the riser is not insulated

20. The try-cocks of steam boilers are used to

   A. act as safety valves
   B. empty the boiler of water
   C. test steam pressure in the boiler
   D. find the height of water in the boiler

21. The MOST important reason for cleaning soot from a boiler is that the

   A. soot blocks the passage of steam from the boiler
   B. soot gets into the boiler room and makes it dirty
   C. soot reduces the heating efficiency of a boiler
   D. pressure of soot is a frequent cause of the cracking of boiler tubes

22. Panic bolts are standard equipment in school buildings. Their MAIN purpose is to

   A. reduce unauthorized opening of doors and closets
   B. allow for easy opening of exit doors of the building
   C. permit rapid removal of screens from windows when a fire occurs
   D. shut storeroom doors automatically to reduce fire hazards

23. The term RPM is GENERALLY used in connection with the

   A. speed of ventilating fans
   B. water capacity of pipe
   C. heating quality of fuel
   D. electrical output of a transformer

24. A hacksaw is a light framed saw MOST commonly used to

   A. cut curved patterns in metal
   B. trim edges
   C. cut wood in confined spaces
   D. cut metal

25. A kilowatt is _____ watts.

   A. 500   B. 2,000   C. 1,500   D. 1,000

KEY (CORRECT ANSWERS)

1.	C	11.	B
2.	C	12.	D
3.	C	13.	C
4.	A	14.	B
5.	A	15.	B
6.	C	16.	D
7.	D	17.	B
8.	D	18.	A
9.	A	19.	B
10.	E	20.	D

21. C
22. B
23. A
24. D
25. D

EXAMINATION SECTION
TEST 1

DIRECTIONS: Each question or incomplete statement is followed by several suggested answers or completions. Select the one that BEST answers the question or completes the statement. *PRINT THE LETTER OF THE CORRECT ANSWER IN THE SPACE AT THE RIGHT.*

1. In the wintertime, the FIRST thing a custodian does in the morning, after throwing the main switch, is to
    A. take a reading of the electric meter
    B. prepare his daily report of fuel consumption
    C. prepare sweeping compound
    D. inspect the water gauge of his boilers

    1.____

2. Rubbish, stones, sticks, and papers on lawns in front of school buildings are MOST effectively collected by means of a
    A. 30 inch floor brush with thickly set bristles
    B. corn broom
    C. 4 foot pole with a nail set in the bottom of it
    D. rake

    2.____

3. Which of the following statements about sweeping is NOT correct?
    A. Corridors and stairs should not be swept during school hours.
    B. Classrooms should usually be swept daily after the close of the afternoon session.
    C. Dry sweeping is not to be used in classrooms or corridors.
    D. Special rooms, as sewing rooms, may be swept during school hours if unoccupied.

    3.____

4. The PROPER size of floor brush to be used in classrooms with fixed seats is _____ inches.
    A. 36   B. 24   C. 16   D. 6

    4.____

5. Sweeping compound made of oiled sawdust should NOT be used on _____ floors.
    A. cement   B. rubber tile
    C. oiled wood   D. composition

    5.____

6. In oiling a wood floor, it is GOOD practice to
    A. apply the oil with a dipped mop up to the baseboards of the walls
    B. avoid application of oil closer than 6 inches of the baseboards
    C. keep the oil about one inch from the baseboard
    D. make sure that oil is applied to the floors under radiators

    6.____

7. Of the following, the LEAST desirable agent for cleaning blackboards is   7.____
   A. damp cloth
   B. clear warm water applied with a sponge
   C. warm water with a little kerosene
   D. warm water containing a mild soap solution

8. Chalk trays of blackboards should be washed and cleaned   8.____
   A. once a week
   B. daily
   C. only when the teacher reports cleaning needed
   D. once a month

9. In cleaning rooms by means of a central vacuum cleaning system,   9.____
   A. sweeping compound is used merely to prevent dust from rising
   B. rooms need cleaning only twice a week because the machine takes up the oil
   C. wood floors must be oiled more frequently as the machine takes up the oil
   D. the cleaner should not press down upon the tool but should guide it across the floor

10. A gas leak is suspected in the home economics class of a school.   10.____
    The procedure in locating the leak is to
    A. use a lighted match
    B. use a safety lamp
    C. place nose close to line and smell each section
    D. use soapsuds

11. The MOST important reason for placing asbestos jackets on steam lines is to   11.____
    A. prevent persons from burning their hands
    B. prevent heat loss
    C. protect the lines from injury
    D. make the lines appear more presentable

12. If the flag is used on a speaker's platform, it should be displayed   12.____
    A. above and behind the speaker
    B. as a drape over the front of the platform
    C. as a rosette over the speaker's head
    D. as a cover over the speaker's desk

13. When the flag of the United States of America is displayed from a staff   13.____
    projecting from the front of the building, it should be
    A. extended to the tip of the staff
    B. extended to about one foot from the tip of the staff
    C. secured so that there is a sag in the line
    D. extended slowly to the tip of the staff and then drawn back rapidly about 15 inches

3 (#1)

14. The common soda-acid fire extinguisher should be checked and refilled 14.____
    A. every week
    B. every month
    C. once a year
    D. only if used

15. A small fire has broken out in an electric motor in a sump pump. The lubricant has apparently caught fire. 15.____
    The PROPER extinguisher to use is
    A. sand
    B. carbon tetrachloride (pyrene) fire extinguisher
    C. soda-acid fire extinguisher
    D. water under pressure from a hose

16. While cleaning windows, an employee falls from the fourth floor of the building to the sidewalk. The custodian finds the man unconscious. 16.____
    The custodian should
    A. move the man into a more comfortable position near the wall of the building and then call a doctor
    B. try to revive the man by depressing his head slightly and applying artificial respiration
    C. hail a taxi and bring the man to a hospital for treatment
    D. phone for an ambulance and cover the man to keep him warm

17. The duties of a custodian include the knowledge of safety rules to prevent accidents and injuries to his employees and himself. 17.____
    Of the following, the LEAST harmful practice is to
    A. carry a scraper in the pocket with the blade down
    B. measure the cleaning powder with your hands before placing the powder in water
    C. wet the hands before using steel wool
    D. use lye to clean paint brushes

18. The MOST important reason for not wringing out a mop by hand is that 18.____
    A. water cannot be removed effectively in this way
    B. it is not fair to the cleaner
    C. the dirt remains on the mop after the water is removed
    D. pins, nail, or other sharp objects may be picked up and cut the hand, causing an infection

19. The method of using a ladder which you would consider LEAST safe is: 19.____
    A. Grasping the side rails of the ladder instead of the rungs when going up
    B. To see that the door is secured wide open when working on a ladder at a door
    C. Leaning weight toward ladder while working on it
    D. Standing on top of the ladder to reach working place

20. When a window pane is broken, the FIRST step the custodian takes is to 20.____
    A. remove broken glass from floors and window sill
    B. determine the cause

C. remove the putty with a putty knife
D. prepare a piece of glass to replace the broken pane

21. Your instructions to a cleaner about the proper sweeping of offices should include the following instruction:
    A. Do not move chairs and wastebaskets from their places when sweeping
    B. Place chairs and baskets on the desks to get them out of the way
    C. Set aside the loose small furniture and chairs in an orderly manner when sweeping office floors
    D. Move the desks and chair to the side of the room close to the wall in order to sweep properly

21.____

22. To remove dirt accumulations after the completion of the sweeping task, brushes should be
    A. tapped on the floor in the normal sweeping position
    B. struck on the floor against the side of the block
    C. struck on the floor against the end of the block
    D. turned upside down and the handle tapped on the floor

22.____

23. To sweep rough cement floors in a basement, the BEST tool to use is a
    A. deck brush   B. new 30" floor brush
    C. corn broom   D. treated mop

23.____

24. When a floor is scrubbed, it is NOT correct to
    A. use a steady, even rotary motion
    B. rinse the floor with clean hot water
    C. have the mop strokes follow the boards when drying the floor
    D. wet the floor first by pouring several bucketsful of water on it

24.____

25. Flushing with a hose is MOST appropriate as a method of cleaning
    A. terrazzo floors of corridors
    B. untreated wood floors
    C. linoleum floor where not in frequent use
    D. cement floors

25.____

KEY (CORRECT ANSWERS)

1.	D		11.	B
2.	D		12.	A
3.	A		13.	A
4.	C		14.	C
5.	B		15.	B
6.	D		16.	D
7.	C		17.	A
8.	A		18.	D
9.	D		19.	D
10.	D		20.	A

21. C
22. A
23. C
24. D
25. D

TEST 2

DIRECTIONS: Each question or incomplete statement is followed by several suggested answers or completions. Select the one that BEST answers the question or completes the statement. *PRINT THE LETTER OF THE CORRECT ANSWER IN THE SPACE AT THE RIGHT.*

Questions 1-5.

DIRECTIONS: Column I lists cleaning jobs. Column II lists cleansing agents and devices. Select the proper cleansing agent from Column II for each job in Column I. Place the letter of the cleansing agent selected in the space at the right corresponding to the number of the cleansing job.

COLUMN I	COLUMN II	
1. Chewing gum	A. Muriatic acid	1.____
2. Ink stains	B. Broad bladed knife	2.____
3. Fingermarks on glass	C. Kerosene	3.____
4. Rust stains on porcelain	D. Oxalic acid	4.____
5. Hardened dirt on porcelain	E. Lye	5.____
	F. Linseed oil	

6. When the bristles of a floor brush have worn short, the brush should be 6.____
   A. thrown away and the handles saved
   B. saved and the brush used on rough cement floors
   C. saved and used for high dusting in classrooms
   D. saved and used for the weekly scrubbing of linoleum floors

7. Feather dusters should NOT be used because they 7.____
   A. take more time to use than other dusters
   B. cannot be cleaned
   C. do not take up the dust but merely move it from one place to another
   D. do not stir up the dust and streak the furniture with dust rails

8. Floors that are usually NOT waxed are those made of 8.____
   A. pine wood   B. mastic tile   C. rubber tile   D. terrazzo

9. For sweeping under radiators and other inaccessible places, the MOST appropriate tool is the 9.____
   A. counter brush   B. dry mop
   C. feather duster   D. 16" floor brush

10. A cleansing agent that should NOT be used in the cleaning of windows is 10.____
    A. water containing fine pumice
    B. water containing a small amount of ammonia
    C. water containing a little kerosene
    D. a paste cleanser made from water and cleaning powder

11. The BEST way to dust desks is to use a 11.____
    A. circular motion with soft dry cloth that has been washed
    B. damp cloth, taking care not to disturb papers on the desk
    C. soft cloth, moistened with oil, using a back and forth motion
    D. back and forth motion with a soft dry cloth

12. Trisodium phosphate is a substance BEST used in 12.____
    A. washing kalsomined walls   B. polishing of brass
    C. washing mastic tile floors   D. clearing stoppages

13. Treated linoleum is PROPERLY cleaned by daily 13.____
    A. dusting with a treated mop
    B. sweeping with a floor brush
    C. mopping with a weak soap solution
    D. mopping after removal of dust with a floor brush

14. Of the following, the MOST proper use for chamois skin is 14.____
    A. drying of window glass after washing
    B. washing of window glass
    C. polishing of metal fixtures
    D. drying toilet bowls after washing

15. A squeegee is a tool which is used in 15.____
    A. clearing stoppage in waste lines
    B. the central vacuum cleaning system
    C. cleaning inside boiler surfaces
    D. drying windows after washing

16. Concrete and cement floors are usually painted a battleship gray color. 16.____
    The MOST important reason for painting the floor is
    A. to improve the appearance of the floor
    B. the paint prevents the absorption of too much water when the floor is mopped
    C. the paint makes the floor safer and less slippery
    D. the concrete becomes harder and will not settle

17. After a sweeping assignment is completed, floor brushes should be stored 17.____
    A. in the normal sweeping position, bristles resting on the floor
    B. by hanging the brushes on pegs or nails
    C. by piling the brushes on each other carefully in a horizontal position
    D. in a dry place after a daily washing

18. Painted walls and ceilings should be brushed down
    A. daily
    B. weekly
    C. every month, especially during the winter
    D. two or three times a year

19. If an asphalt tile floor becomes excessively dirty, the method of cleaning should include
    A. the use of kerosene or benzene as a solvent
    B. the use of a solution of modified laundry soda
    C. sanding down the spotted areas with a sanding machine on the wet floor
    D. use of a light oil and treated mop

20. To remove light stains from marble walls, the BEST method is to
    A. use steel wool and a scouring powder, then rinse with clear warm water
    B. wash the stained area with a dilute acid solution
    C. sand down the spot first, then wash with mild soap solution
    D. wet marble first, then scrub with mild soap solution using a soft fiber brush

21. To rid a toilet room of objectionable odors, the PROPER method is to
    A. spread some chloride of lime on the floor
    B. place deodorizer cubes in a box hung on the wall
    C. wash the floor with hot water containing a little kerosene
    D. wash the floor with hot water into which some disinfectant has been poured

22. Toilet rooms, to be cleaned properly, should be swept
    A. daily
    B. and mopped daily
    C. daily and mopped twice a week
    D. daily and mopped thoroughly at the end of the week

23. In waxing a floor, it is usually BEST to
    A. start the waxing under stationary furniture and then do the aisles
    B. pour the wax on the floor, spreading it under the desks with a wax mop
    C. remove the old wax coat before rewaxing
    D. wet mop the floor after the second coat has dried to obtain a high polish

24. The BEST reason why water should not be used to clean kalsomined walls of a boiler room is that the
    A. walls are usually not smooth and will hold too much water
    B. kalsomine coating does not hold dust
    C. kalsomine coating will dissolve in water and leave streaks
    D. wall brick and kalsomine coating will not dissolve in water and so cannot be cleaned

25. In mopping a floor, it is BEST practice to 25._____
    A. swing the mop from side to side, using the widest possible stroke across the floor up to the baseboard
    B. swing the mop from side to side, using the widest possible stroke across the floor surface, stopping the stroke from 3 to 5 inches from baseboards
    C. use short, straight strokes, up and back, stopping the strokes about 5 inches from the baseboard
    D. use short straight strokes, up and back, stopping the strokes at the baseboards

KEY (CORRECT ANSWERS)

1.	B	11.	D
2.	D	12.	C
3.	C	13.	A
4.	A	14.	A
5.	C	15.	D
6.	B	16.	B
7.	C	17.	B
8.	D	18.	D
9.	A	19.	D
10.	A	20.	D

21.	D
22.	B
23.	A
24.	C
25.	B

EXAMINATION SECTION
TEST 1

DIRECTIONS: Each question or incomplete statement is followed by several suggested answers or completions. Select the one that BEST answers the question or completes the statement. *PRINT THE LETTER OF THE CORRECT ANSWER IN THE SPACE AT THE RIGHT.*

1. Of the following, the BEST way for you to make sure that a cleaner understands a spoken order which you have given to him is for you to

    A. ask him to repeat the order in his own words
    B. ask him whether he has understood the order
    C. watch how he begins to follow the order
    D. ask him whether he has any questions about the order

1.____

2. You have called a meeting with your cleaners to get their suggestions on ways to keep up cleaning standards in spite of budget cutbacks.
You are MOST likely to be successful in encouraging them to participate in the discussion if you

    A. start the meeting by giving the cleaners all your own suggestions first
    B. keep the meeting going by talking whenever the cleaners have nothing to say
    C. get the cleaners to *think out loud* by asking them for their interpretations of the problem
    D. comment on and evaluate the suggestions made by each cleaner immediately after he makes them

2.____

3. If a custodian knows that rumors being spread by his assistants are false, he should

    A. tell the assistants that the rumors are false
    B. tell the assistants the facts which the rumors have falsified
    C. threaten to discipline any assistant who spreads the rumors
    D. find out which assistant started the rumor and have him suspended

3.____

4. One of your best cleaners tells you in private that he wants to quit his job.
The FIRST thing you should do in handling this matter is to

    A. ask the cleaner why he wants to quit his job
    B. tell the cleaner to take a few days to think it over
    C. refer the cleaner to the personnel office
    D. try to convince the cleaner not to quit his job

4.____

5. The MOST important reason why a custodian should seek the suggestions of his cleaners on job-related matters is that the

    A. cleaners generally have greater knowledge of job-related matters than the custodian
    B. cleaners will tend to have a greater feeling of participation in their jobs by making suggestions
    C. custodian will be able to hold the cleaners responsible for any suggestions he follows
    D. custodian can win the respect of his cleaners by showing them the errors in their suggestions

5.____

6. Your supervisor has ordered you to announce to your cleaners a new cleaning rule with which you disagree. You should

   A. admit honestly to your cleaners that you disagree with the rule
   B. announce the rule to your cleaners without expressing your disagreement
   C. encourage your cleaners by telling them you agree with the rule
   D. tell your supervisor that you refuse to announce any rule with which you disagree

7. Of the following, the BEST practice to follow in criticizing the work performance of a cleaner is to

   A. save up several criticisms and make them all at one time
   B. soften your criticisms by being humorous
   C. have another cleaner, who has more seniority, give the criticism
   D. make sure you explain to the cleaner the reasons for your criticism

8. The work goals which you set for your cleaners should be

   A. slightly less than their capabilities, so that they have some slack time
   B. approximately equal to their capabilities, so that they work at normal capacity
   C. slightly above their capabilities, so that they must extend themselves a little
   D. considerably above their capabilities, so that they must always be trying to catch up

9. Of the following, the BEST way to reduce unnecessary absences among your cleaners is to

   A. ask your cleaners the reason for their absence every time they are absent
   B. rely entirely on written warnings once every month to cleaners who have been absent too often during the month
   C. have your cleaners make a formal written report to you every time they are absent explaining the reason for their absence
   D. post publicly every month a list of those cleaners who you feel have been absent unnecessarily during the month

10. Of the following methods that might be used to deal with a cleaner who is habitually late for work without good reason, the BEST one for you to apply is to

    A. give the cleaner an assignment where his lateness will not inconvenience any other cleaner
    B. assign the cleaner to the most disagreeable jobs until he stops being late for work
    C. call the cleaner aside in private to give him a stern lecture on his habitual lateness
    D. appeal to the cleaner's better nature to urge him to correct his habitual lateness

11. To improve efficiency, you have instituted a new system of assigning work to your cleaners.
    Your cleaners are MOST likely to be cooperative in accepting this new system if you

    A. remind them how inefficient the former system was
    B. tell them of the advantages of the new system but not the disadvantages
    C. refuse to make any changes in the new system once you have instituted it
    D. follow-up on any problems the cleaners may have because of the new system

12. You are most likely to gain the wholehearted cooperation of your cleaners if you appeal MAINLY to their

   A. natural dislike for work
   B. fear of punishment
   C. satisfaction in a job well done
   D. desire to avoid responsibility

13. When combined with good leadership, regular inspections by a custodian of the work done by his cleaners can help create good morale MAINLY because the cleaners know that the custodian

   A. is interested in how they do their work
   B. will leave them alone between inspections
   C. may catch them if they do poor work
   D. does not rely on them to do their work unwatched

14. While you are making an inspection, you find two of your cleaners arguing angrily about the best procedure to follow in completing their assignment.
    Of the following, the FIRST thing you should do is to

   A. tell them that they will both be disciplined
   B. ignore the argument, since it is probably none of your business
   C. ask each one for his side of the argument
   D. order them to follow the procedure favored by the more experienced of the two

15. A one-person cleaning assignment which all of your cleaners find disagreeable comes up one day every month. It is BEST supervisory practice to assign

   A. each one in turn, by rotation
   B. anyone who happens to be available, by chance
   C. anyone you wish to punish for his poor work performance
   D. the one who is least likely to complain about the assignment

16. Despite your repeated warnings, one of your cleaners, through carelessness, has seriously damaged an expensive waxing machine.
    You are MOST likely to be effective in disciplining him if you

   A. reprimand him in the presence of the other cleaners
   B. consider his work record when deciding how to discipline him
   C. tell him that you will decide on a punishment for him during the following week
   D. make a point of reminding him frequently how he carelessly damaged an expensive waxing machine

17. A custodian is approached by a newspaper reporter and is asked questions about a certain member of the office staff. Of the following, the BEST course of action for the custodian to take is to

   A. ignore the newspaper reporter
   B. refer the newspaper reporter to the personnel office for information
   C. tell the newspaper reporter anything he wishes to know, but warn him that the information is not official
   D. give the newspaper reporter false information to discourage further questioning

18. While a custodian is making a note of the fluorescent lamps that need to be replaced in a waiting room, one of the waiting clients starts to complain angrily about the high cost of custodial services in the city.
Of the following, the BEST course of action for the custodian to take is to

    A. tell the individual to be quiet and show more respect for city representatives
    B. try to persuade the person to take a more reasonable point of view
    C. listen courteously until the client has finished and then complain about the high cost of welfare
    D. ignore the comments and continue with his work

19. A group of workers complain to you about the lack of cleanliness in your building. You realize that budget cutbacks have unavoidably led to shortages in manpower and equipment for the cleaning staff.
Of the following, the BEST way for you to answer these workers is to

    A. tell them frankly that the cleanliness of the building is none of their business
    B. apologize for the condition of the building and promise that your men will work harder
    C. tell them to take their complaints to the administration and not to you
    D. explain the reasons for the building's condition and what you are doing to improve it

20. The MOST important role of the custodian in promoting good public relations should be to help

    A. increase understanding between the custodial staff and the public which it serves
    B. keep from public attention any failings on the part of the custodial staff
    C. increase the authority of the custodial staff over the public with which it deals
    D. keep the public from interfering in the operations of the custodial staff

21. A supervisor conducting a staff meeting calls you to complain that the cleaners working in the empty office next to his are being unnecessarily noisy.
Of the following, the BEST response to the supervisor is to tell him that

    A. he should go next door to tell the cleaners to stop the unnecessary noise
    B. you will tell the cleaners about his complaint and instruct them not to make unnecessary noise
    C. he should file a formal complaint against the cleaners with your superior
    D. you will come to his office to judge for yourself whether the cleaners are being unnecessarily noisy

22. The attitude a custodian should *generally* maintain toward the workers and office staff is one of

    A. avoidance   B. superiority
    C. courtesy   D. servility

23. A custodian notices that one of the clerks in using an unsafe electrical appliance which may cause a fire at any time.
    Of the following, the BEST course of action for the custodian to take is to

    A. go into the clerk's office after hours and remove the appliance
    B. notify the fire department so that a summons will be served on the clerk
    C. go into the clerk's office after hours and damage the appliance in such a way as to eliminate the hazard
    D. speak to the clerk's supervisor privately and explain the danger and request that the supervisor ask the clerk to disconnect the appliance

23._____

24. An emergency has developed in which a custodian must enter a locked office to close some shut-off valves. The occupant of the office is a new employee who is alone and refuses to let the custodian in because she does not recognize him.
    Of the following, the BEST course of action for the custodian to take is to

    A. force his way in and then apologize
    B. summon the police and explain that she is obstructing official city business
    C. show his credentials or seek out other individuals that the employee knows
    D. tell the employee that there is a fire in the building and her life is in danger

24._____

25. A telephone caller tells a building custodian that a bomb has been placed in the building and immediately hangs up the phone.
    The FIRST thing the building custodian should do is to

    A. call the fire department
    B. call the police department
    C. let his subordinate handle it
    D. ignore the call, since most threats are hoaxes

25._____

6 (#1)

KEY (CORRECT ANSWERS)

1. A
2. C
3. B
4. A
5. B

6. B
7. D
8. C
9. A
10. C

11. D
12. C
13. A
14. C
15. A

16. B
17. B
18. D
19. D
20. A

21. B
22. C
23. D
24. C
25. B

TEST 2

DIRECTIONS: Each question or incomplete statement is followed by several suggested answers or completions. Select the one that BEST answers the question or completes the statement. *PRINT THE LETTER OF THE CORRECT ANSWER IN THE SPACE AT THE RIGHT.*

1. Despite your repeated warnings, one of your custodial assistants, through carelessness, has seriously damaged an expensive paper shredder.
   You are MOST likely to be LEAST effective in disciplining him if you

    A. reprimand him in the presence of other custodial assistants
    B. consider his work record when deciding how to discipline him
    C. tell him that you will decide on a punishment for him during the following week
    D. make a point of reminding him now and then how he carelessly damaged an expensive paper shredder

   1._____

2. Assume that one of your custodial assistants, although he does not drink on the job, is an alcoholic whose work performance has become inadequate because of his drinking problem.
   Of the following, the BEST approach to take in dealing with this custodial assistant is to

    A. do nothing, since he does not drink on the job
    B. recommend to your supervisor that the custodial assistant be fired because he is an alcoholic
    C. counsel him on the personal and emotional problems which cause his drinking problem
    D. advise him to seek professional help for his drinking problem

   2._____

3. Of the following, you are MOST likely to be effective in training an inexperienced custodial assistant to do a complicated cleaning job if you

    A. train him in all parts of the job at the same time
    B. first demonstrate to him the most common errors in doing the job
    C. let him know from time to time how he is doing in learning the job
    D. encourage him in the beginning by overlooking any mistakes he may make

   3._____

4. Praising a trainee who is making unusually good progress in learning from your training is *generally* considered to be

    A. *desirable,* because he is likely to be encouraged to continue making good progress
    B. *undesirable,* because he is likely to become overconfident and begin to do poorly
    C. *desirable,* because the other trainees are likely to become envious and try to compete with him
    D. *undesirable,* because he should not be praised for doing his job

   4._____

5. Of the following, the MOST effective way for you to train a custodial assistant to perform a complicated cleaning job about which he has some knowledge is to

    A. let him do the entire job, then have him question you as to his problems
    B. repeat in your training what he already knows about the cleaning job
    C. teach him those parts of the job with which he is unfamiliar
    D. keep him slightly ill at ease during training

   5._____

89

6. A custodial foreman in a large building should *normally* spend the GREATEST part of his working time on

   A. work planning
   B. records and reports
   C. personnel problems
   D. supervision and inspection

7. In general, the MOST efficient method for doing a cleaning job is the method which

   A. must be repeated most frequently
   B. has the most different steps and operations
   C. gives the best results for the least amount of effort
   D. requires the efforts of the greatest number of custodial assistants

8. If the directions given by your superior are not clear, the BEST thing for you to do is to

   A. ask to have the directions repeated and clarified
   B. proceed to do the work taking a chance on doing the right thing
   C. do nothing until some later time when you can find out exactly what is wanted
   D. ask one of the other men in your crew what he would do under the circumstances

9. Of the following procedures concerning grievances of subordinate personnel, the custodian-engineer should maintain an attitude of

   A. paying little attention to little grievances
   B. being very alert to grievances and make adjustments in existing conditions to appease all personnel
   C. knowing the most frequent causes of grievances and strive to prevent them from arising
   D. maintain rigid discipline of a nature that *smooths out* all grievances

10. Of the following, the BEST course of action to take to settle a dispute or conflict between two employees is to

    A. insist that the two employees settle the case between themselves
    B. call in each one separately and, after hearing their cases presented, decide the issue
    C. bring both in for a conference at the same time and make the decision in their presence
    D. have both present their points of view and arguments in written memoranda and on this basis make your decision

11. If, as a custodian-engineer, you discover an error in your report submitted to the main office, you should

    A. do nothing, since it is possible that one error will have little effect on the total report
    B. wait until the error is discovered in the main office and then offer to work overtime to correct it
    C. go directly to the supervisor in the main office after working hours and ask him unofficially to correct the error
    D. notify the main office immediately so that the error can be corrected, if necessary

12. There are a considerable number of forms and reports to be submitted on schedule by the custodian-engineer. The ADVISABLE method of accomplishing this duty is to

    A. fill out the reports at odd times during the days when you have free time
    B. schedule a definite period of the work-week for completing these forms and reports
    C. assign your foreman or cleaner to handle all these forms for you and to have them available on time
    D. classify or group the forms and reports and fill out only one of each group and refer the other forms or reports to the ones completed

13. A custodian-engineer can BEST evaluate the quality of work performed by custodial personnel by

    A. periodic inspection of the building's cleanliness
    B. studying the time records of personnel
    C. reviewing the building cleaning expenditures
    D. analyzing complaints of building occupants

14. Assume that you are the custodian-engineer and one of your employees wants to talk with you about a grievance. Of the following actions, the LEAST desirable action for you to take is to

    A. listen sympathetically
    B. conduct the discussion openly in the presence of the work-force
    C. try to get his point of view
    D. endeavor to obtain all the facts

15. Of the following factors, the one which is LEAST important in evaluating an employee and his work is his

    A. dependability   B. quantity of work
    C. quality of work   D. education and training

16. Supervision of a group of people engaged in building cleaning operations should NOT include supervision of

    A. time spent in cleaning operations
    B. utilization of official rest and lunch periods
    C. cleaning methods
    D. materials used for various cleaning jobs

17. Of the following methods, the BEST one to utilize in assigning custodial personnel to clean a multi-floor school building is to

    A. allow the cleaners to pick their rooms or area assignments out of a hat
    B. have the supervisor make specific room or area assignments to each cleaner separately
    C. rotate room and area assignments daily according to a chart posted on the bulletin board
    D. let a different member of the group make the room or area assignments each week

18. Assume that you are the custodian-engineer and that you have discovered a bottle of liquor in one of your employees' locker.
    The BEST course of action to take is to

A. fire him immediately
B. explain to him that liquor should not be brought into a school building and that a repetition may result in disciplinary action
C. suspend him until the end of the week and take him back only on a probational basis
D. assemble the staff and tell them they are all equally guilty for not having reported the matter to you

19. Of the following items, the one which is the LEAST important in the preparation of a report is that the report 19.____

   A. is brief, but to the point
   B. uses the prescribed form if there is one
   C. contains extra copies
   D. is accurate

20. In order to have building employees willing to follow standardized cleaning and maintenance procedures, the supervisor must be prepared to 20.____

   A. work alongside the employees
   B. demonstrate the reasonableness of the procedures
   C. offer incentive pay for their utilization
   D. allow the employees the free use of the time saved by their adoption

21. A fireman is frequently late in taking over his shift. In considering this situation, the factor which is of LEAST importance is 21.____

   A. the reason for his lateness
   B. how his lateness affects the work of other firemen
   C. how often he is late
   D. how willing he is to do emergency work

22. Suppose that you are preparing a requisition for cleaning supplies for the school year. The BEST single method of estimating the amount to be ordered is to 22.____

   A. ask each cleaner to submit an estimate of his needs for the coming year
   B. call other custodian-engineers to obtain from them an estimate of supply requirements
   C. confer with the school principal to obtain his estimate of school cleaning supply needs
   D. review the records of supplies used during the last few years

23. A number of injuries to pupils have occurred while they were traveling on the stairs of the school. Your inspection shows no defects or inadequacy of lighting. 23.____
The MOST desirable step to take to reduce the frequency of these accidents is to

   A. assign a cleaner to each stairway during the time the children use them
   B. put up signs warning the children to be careful
   C. suggest to the school principal that his teaching staff discuss the matter with the children
   D. install better lighting on the stairs and make certain that handrails are in perfect condition

24. The custodian-engineer, to be effective and efficient, must budget his time. This means MOST NEARLY that

    A. a value in dollars and costs should be placed on each hour's work of a custodian-engineer
    B. the custodian-engineer should make certain that all of his time, as well as that of his employees, is accounted for
    C. a time schedule for each employee must be prepared so that the yearly allowance for the school is not exceeded
    D. the custodian-engineer should plan his jobs and duties so that all can be covered as required

25. Suppose that a cleaner has been found to be quite negligent in his work and has been warned repeatedly by you.
    If you find that your warnings have not changed the man's attitude or work habits, the PROPER thing to do is to

    A. have the employee discharged
    B. change his assignment in the school to a less desirable job
    C. have a serious talk with the cleaner to find out why he does not do satisfactory work
    D. give the cleaner a final warning

KEY (CORRECT ANSWERS)

1.	A		11.	D
2.	D		12.	B
3.	C		13.	A
4.	A		14.	B
5.	C		15.	D
6.	D		16.	B
7.	C		17.	B
8.	A		18.	B
9.	C		19.	C
10.	C		20.	B

21. D
22. D
23. C
24. D
25. A

READING COMPREHENSION
UNDERSTANDING AND INTERPRETING WRITTEN MATERIAL

EXAMINATION SECTION
TEST 1

DIRECTIONS: Each question or incomplete statement is followed by several suggested answers or completions. Select the one that BEST answers the question or completes the statement. *PRINT THE LETTER OF THE CORRECT ANSWER IN THE SPACE AT THE RIGHT.*

Questions 1-3.

DIRECTIONS: Questions 1 through 3 are to be answered in accordance with the following passage.

Terrazzo flooring will last a very long time if it is cared for properly. Lacquers, shellac, or varnish preparations should never be used on terrazzo. Soap cleaners are not recommended since they dull the appearance of the floor. Alkaline solutions are harmful, so a neutral cleaner or non-alkaline synthetic detergents will give best results. If the floor is very dirty, it may be necessary to scrub it. The same neutral cleaning solution should be used for scrubbing as for mopping. Scouring powder may be sprinkled at particularly dirty spots. Do not use steel wool for scrubbing. Small pieces of steel filings left on the floor will rust and dis-color the terrazzo. Non-woven nylon or open-mesh fabric abrasive pads are suitable for scrubbing terrazzo floors.

1. According to the passage above, the BEST cleaning agent for terrazzo flooring is a(n) 1.____

   A. soap cleaner B. varnish preparation
   C. neutral cleaner D. alkaline solution

2. According to the passage above, terrazzo floors should NOT be scrubbed with 2.____

   A. non-woven nylon abrasive pads
   B. steel wool
   C. open-mesh fabric abrasive pads
   D. scouring powder

3. As used in the passage above, the word *discolor* means MOST NEARLY 3.____

   A. crack   B. scratch   C. dissolve   D. stain

Questions 4-7.

DIRECTIONS: Questions 4 through 7 are to be answered in accordance with the information given in the following passage.

MOPPING FLOORS

When mopping hardened cement floors, either painted or unpainted, a soap and water mixture should be used. This should be made by dissolving half a cup of soft soap in a pail of hot water. It is not desirable, however, under any circumstances, to use a soap and water mixture on cement floors that are not hardened. For mopping this type of floor, it is recommended that the cleaning agent be made up of 2 ounces of laundry soda mixed in a pail of water.

Soaps are not generally used on hard tile floors because slippery films may build up on the floor. It is generally recommended that these floors be mopped using a pail of hot water in which has been mixed 2 ounces of washing powder for each gallon of water. The floors should then be rinsed thoroughly.

After the mopping is finished, proper care should be taken of the mop. This is done by first cleaning the mop in clear warm water. Then, it should be wrung out, after which the strands of the mop should be untangled. Finally, the mop should be hung by its handle to dry.

4. According to the above passage, you should NEVER use a soap and water mixture when mopping _____ floors.

   A. hardened cement
   B. painted
   C. unhardened cement
   D. unpainted

5. According to the above passage, using laundry soda mixed in a pail of water as a cleaning agent is recommended for

   A. all floors
   B. all floors except hard tile floors
   C. some cement floors
   D. linoleum floor coverings *only*

6. According to the above passage, the GENERALLY recommended mixture for mopping hard tile floors is _____ of hot water.

   A. 1/2 cup of soft soap for each gallon
   B. 1/2 cup of soft soap in a pail
   C. 2 ounces of washing powder in a pail
   D. 2 ounces of washing powder for each gallon

7. According to the above passage, the PROPER care of a mop after it is used includes

   A. cleaning it in clear cold water and hanging it by its handle to dry
   B. wringing it out, untangling and drying it
   C. untangling its strands before wringing it out
   D. untangling its strands while cleaning it in clear water

Questions 8-15.

DIRECTIONS: Questions 8 through 15 are to be answered ONLY in accordance with the following paragraph.

Many custodial foremen have discovered through experience that there are economies to be *realized* by using discretion when ordering items which are similar to each other. For example, it may be cheaper to order a *Sponge block, cellulose, WET SIZE: 6 in. x 4 3/4 in. x APPROXIMATELY 34 inches long* at $7.00 than it is to order separate *Sponges, cellulose, wet size: 2 in. x 4 in. x 6 in.* at 60¢. It does not pay to *over-order* on floor wax which may turn sour if not used soon enough. An average size college building cannot afford to have extra 30-inch floor brooms costing $19.75 each stored *on the shelf* for a couple of years or to let moths destroy the hair in such brooms if proper safeguards are not used.

8. According to the above passage, the items mentioned which are *similar* are

    A. floor brooms
    B. sponges
    C. floor waxes
    D. moths

9. As used in the above paragraph, the term *over-order* means to

    A. order again
    B. back order
    C. order too little
    D. order too much

10. Of the items for which prices are given in the above paragraph, the MOST expensive one is the

    A. 30-inch floor broom
    B. 6 in. x 4 3/4 in. x 34 in. sponge block
    C. 2 in. x 4 in. x 6 in. sponge
    D. floor wax

11. As used in the above paragraph, the word *realized* means MOST NEARLY

    A. obtained   B. lost   C. equalized   D. cheapened

12. According to the above paragraph, the one of the following which may be damaged by moths is the

    A. floor broom
    B. sponge
    C. cellulose
    D. wool cloth

13. As used in the above paragraph, the term *wet size* means

    A. the chemical treatment given to sponges
    B. the amount of water the sponge can hold
    C. that the sponges must be kept moist at all times
    D. that the measurements given were taken when the sponges were wet

14. As used in the above paragraph, the word *at* means

    A. near   B. arrived   C. each   D. new

15. As used in the above paragraph, the word *approximately* means

    A. exactly   B. about   C. economical   D. tan

Questions 16-17.

DIRECTIONS: Questions 16 and 17 are to be answered in accordance with the following paragraph.

Painting is done to preserve surfaces; and unless the surface is properly prepared, good preservation will not be possible. Apply paint only to clean dry surfaces. After a surface has been scaled, which means that all loose paint and rust are removed by chipping, scraping, and wire brushing, be sure all dust and dirt are completely removed.

16. According to the above paragraph, the MAIN purpose of painting a wall is to _____ the wall.

    A. clean
    B. waterproof
    C. protect
    D. remove dust from

17. According to the above paragraph,

    A. chipping, scraping, and wire brushing are the only methods permitted for cleaning surfaces
    B. painting is effective only when the surface is clean
    C. scaling refers only to the removal of rust
    D. paint may be applied on wet surfaces

Questions 18-21.

DIRECTIONS: Questions 18 through 21 are to be answered SOLELY on the basis of the following paragraph.

All cleaning agents and supplies should be kept in a central storeroom which should be kept locked and only the custodian, store-keeper, and foreman should have keys. Shelving should be provided for the smaller items while barrels containing scouring powder or other bulk material should be set on the floor or on special cradles. Each compartment in the shelves should be marked plainly and only the item indicated stored therein. Each barrel should also be marked plainly. It may also be desirable to keep special items such as electric lamps, flashlight batteries, etc. in a locked cabinet or separate room to which only the custodian and the night building foreman have keys.

18. According to the above paragraph, scouring powder

    A. should be kept on shelves
    B. comes in one-pound cans
    C. should be kept in a locked cabinet
    D. is a bulk material

19. According to the above paragraph,

    A. the storekeeper should not be entrusted with the safekeeping of light bulbs
    B. flashlight batteries should be stored in barrels
    C. the central storeroom should be kept locked
    D. only special items should be stored under lock and key

20. According to the above paragraph,

    A. each shelf compartment should contain at least four different items
    B. barrels must be stored in cradles
    C. all items stored should be in marked compartments
    D. crates of light bulbs should be stored in cradles

21. As used in the above paragraph, the word *cradle* means a 21.____

    A. dolly
    B. support
    C. doll's bed
    D. hand truck

Questions 22-25.

DIRECTIONS: Questions 22 through 25 are to be answered SOLELY on the basis of the following paragraph.

There are on the market many cleaning agents for which amazing claims are made. Chemical analysis shows that the majority of them are well-known chemicals slightly modified and packaged and sold under various trade names. For that reason, the agents which have been selected for your use are those whose cleaning properties are well-known and whose use can be standardized. It is obviously undesirable to offer too wide a selection as that would be confusing to the cleaner, but a sufficient number must be provided so that a satisfactory agent is available for each task.

22. According to the above paragraph, 22.____

    A. there are few cleaning agents on the market
    B. there are no really good cleaning agents on the market
    C. cleaning agents are sold under several different brand names
    D. all cleaning agents are the same

23. According to the above paragraph, 23.____

    A. all cleaning agents should be chemically analyzed before use
    B. the best cleaning agents are those for which no claims are made by the manufacturer
    C. different cleaning agents may be needed for different tasks
    D. all cleaning agents have been standardized by the federal government

24. As used in the above paragraph, the word *amazing* means 24.____

    A. illegal
    B. untrue
    C. astonishing
    D. specific

25. As used in the above paragraph, the word *modified* means 25.____

    A. changed   B. refined   C. labelled   D. diluted

KEY (CORRECT ANSWERS)

1. C
2. B
3. D
4. C
5. C

6. D
7. B
8. B
9. D
10. A

11. A
12. A
13. D
14. C
15. B

16. C
17. B
18. D
19. C
20. C

21. B
22. C
23. C
24. C
25. A

TEST 2

Questions 1-3.

DIRECTIONS: Questions 1 through 3 are to be answered in accordance with the following passage. Each question or incomplete statement is followed by several suggested answers or completions. Select the one that BEST answers the question or completes the statement. *PRINT THE LETTER OF THE CORRECT ANSWER IN THE SPACE AT THE RIGHT.*

The method of cleaning which should generally be used is the space assignment method. Under this method, the buildings to be cleaned are divided into different sections. Within each section, each crew of Custodial Assistants is assigned to do one particular cleaning job. For example, within a section, one crew may be assigned to cleaning offices, another to scrubbing floors, a third to collecting trash, and so on. Other methods which may be used are the post assignment method and the gang cleaning method. Under the post assignment method, a Custodial Assistant is assigned to one area of a building and performs all cleaning jobs in that area. This method is seldom used except where buildings are so small and distant from each other that it is not economical to use the space assignment method. Under the gang cleaning method, a Custodial Foreman takes a number of Custodial Assistants through a section of the building. These Custodial Assistants work as a group and complete the various cleaning jobs as they go. This method is generally used only where the building contains very large open areas.

1. According to the passage above, under the space assignment method, each crew GENERALLY

   A. works as a group and does a variety of different cleaning jobs
   B. is assigned to one area and performs all cleaning jobs in that area
   C. does one particular cleaning job within a section of a building
   D. follows the Custodial Foreman through a building containing large, open areas

   1.____

2. According to the passage above, the post assignment method is used MOSTLY where the buildings to be cleaned are _____ in size and situated _____.

   A. large; close together   B. small; close together
   C. large; far apart   D. small; far apart

   2.____

3. As used in the passage above, the word *economical* means MOST NEARLY

   A. thrifty   B. agreed   C. unusual   D. wasteful

   3.____

Questions 4-25.

DIRECTIONS: Each question consists of a statement. You are to indicate whether the statement is TRUE (T) or FALSE (F). *PRINT THE LETTER OF THE CORRECT ANSWER IN THE SPACE AT THE RIGHT.*

Questions 4-8.

DIRECTIONS: Questions 4 through 8 are to be answered in accordance with the information given in the following paragraph.

The removal of fine, loose dirt or dust from desks, chairs, filing cabinets, tables, and other furniture or office machines is called dusting. A yard of clean soft cloth, folded into a pad about nine inches square, is best for dusting. The cloth should be dry since oil or water on the cloth may streak the surface that is being dusted. When dusting a desk, care must be taken to put back in the same place any papers that were lifted or moved to one side. Thorough dusting of an office is important in order for the office to look neat and for the health of the people who work in that office.

4. The removal of fine, loose dirt or dust from furniture or office machines is called dusting.   4._____

5. A pad of cloth twelve inches square is best for dusting.   5._____

6. A dry cloth will streak the surface that is being dusted.   6._____

7. Papers that have been lifted or moved to one side when dusting a desk should be put back in the same place.   7._____

8. It is not important to dust an office thoroughly.   8._____

Questions 9-18.

DIRECTIONS: Questions 9 through 18 are to be answered in accordance with the information given in the following paragraphs.

WASHING OF WALLS

The washing of walls is important since wall-cleaning costs are an expensive item in the operating cost of building maintenance.

There is a right and a wrong way to wash walls. Streaks may be caused by water running down the dry wall below the place where one is working. This can be prevented by first wetting a section of the wall with water, starting at the bottom and working up before starting the actual washing operation with cleaning solution. Then, if the water runs down the wet wall, there will be almost no streaking. While washing a wall, the temperature should be reasonably low so that the water will not dry on the wall and cause streaks. Once the dirt on the wall is moistened, the wall must be kept wet until the dirt is removed. The washing of walls should be done with good sponges. One sponge should be for cleaning on the dirty wall and one for rinsing.

When working with the cleaning solution, start at the top of the wall and use a circular motion of the sponge and hand. Work across a given section first to the right and then to the left, and so on down to the base.

After the dirt has been removed, take clean, cool water and a clean sponge and go over the wall to be sure that it is perfectly clean and that no traces of the cleaning solution remain on the wall. Even clean water drying unevenly on a wall will cause slight streaks which become noticeable on the walls.

9. The amount of money spent to wash walls is a very small part in the expenses of running a building.   9._____

10. To prevent streaks when washing a wall, an employee should FIRST wet the wall, starting at the top and working down to the base of a wall.

11. If a wall is wet in the right way, there will be practically no streaks caused by water running down the wet wall.

12. If the walls are washed when the room is hot, streaks can be caused by water drying too quickly.

13. Once a dirty wall is made wet with water, it should be dried completely before the dirt is removed.

14. To wash walls properly, an employee should use at least two good sponges.

15. When washing with the cleaning solution, start at the bottom of the wall and work to the top, using a circular motion of the hand and sponge.

16. When washing with the cleaning solution, the CORRECT method is to work across each part of the wall going first to the left and ending on the right.

17. After the wall has been washed with the cleaning solution, it must be gone over again with clean water to remove any solution which is left on the wall.

18. When clean water is used to wash a wall, streaks will never appear, even if the wall dries unevenly.

Questions 19-25.

DIRECTIONS: Questions 19 through 25 are to be answered in accordance with the information given in the following passage.

CLEANING ELECTRIC LIGHT FIXTURES

A room may be dark not because there are not enough light fixtures but because the globes are dirty. As frequently as found necessary, and at least once a year, each globe on a light fixture should be taken down and carefully washed. It should be cleaned by using a solution of warm water to which has been added about two tablespoons full of washing soda for each 10 quarts of water. The globe must be thoroughly dried before it is put back or it is liable to crack from the heat of the lamp. At the time the globe is washed, the metal parts of the fixture should be wiped with a rag dampened in plain warm water. Most metal fixtures have been lacquered, and any cleaning solution would tend to destroy the lacquer. The electric light bulb should be unscrewed from the fixture and wiped with a slighly damp cloth. If it is burned out, it should be replaced at this time.

19. Dirty light globes will reduce the amount of light in a room.

20. Light globes should be cleaned only when the attendant replaces a burned out light bulb in a fixture.

21. To clean light globes, a solution of cold water and ordinary household ammonia should be used.

22. If a light globe is not completely dry when it is put back on a fixture after washing, the heat from the light bulb can break the globe.   22._____

23. The metal parts of a light fixture should be cleaned by using a dry rag to which has been added a few drops of a cleaning solution.   23._____

24. Most metal light fixtures have a coating of lacquer on them.   24._____

25. To clean a light bulb in a fixture, it should be unscrewed and wiped with a damp cloth.   25._____

KEY (CORRECT ANSWERS)

1.	C	11.	T
2.	D	12.	T
3.	A	13.	F
4.	T	14.	T
5.	F	15.	F
6.	F	16.	F
7.	T	17.	T
8.	F	18.	F
9.	F	19.	T
10.	F	20.	F

21. F
22. T
23. F
24. T
25. T

SUPERVISION STUDY GUIDE

Social science has developed information about groups and leadership in general and supervisor-employee relationships in particular. Since organizational effectiveness is closely linked to the ability of supervisors to direct the activities of employees, these findings are important to executives everywhere.

IS A SUPERVISOR A LEADER?

First-line supervisors are found in all large business and government organizations. They are the men at the base of an organizational hierarchy. Decisions made by the head of the organization reach them through a network of intermediate positions. They are frequently referred to as part of the management team, but their duties seldom seem to support this description.

A supervisor of clerks, tax collectors, meat inspectors, or securities analysts is not charged with budget preparation. He cannot hire or fire the employees in his own unit on his say-so. He does not administer programs which require great planning, coordinating, or decision making.

Then what is he? He is the man who is directly in charge of a group of employees doing productive work for a business or government agency. If the work requires the use of machines, the men he supervises operate them. If the work requires the writing of reports, the men he supervises write them. He is expected to maintain a productive flow of work without creating problems which higher levels of management must solve. But is he a leader?

To carry out a specific part of an agency's mission, management creates a unit, staffs it with a group of employees and designates a supervisor to take charge of them. Management directs what this unit shall do, from time to time changes directions, and often indicates what the group should not do. Management presumably creates status for the supervisor by giving him more pay, a title, and special privileges.

Management asks a supervisor to get his workers to attain organizational goals, including the desired quantity and quality of production. Supposedly, he has authority to enable him to achieve this objective. Management at least assumes that by establishing the status of the supervisor's position, it has created sufficient authority to enable him to achieve these goals— not his goals, nor necessarily the group's, but management's goals.

In addition, supervision includes writing reports, keeping records of membership in a higher-level administrative group, industrial engineering, safety engineering, editorial duties, housekeeping duties, etc. The supervisor as a member of an organizational network, must be responsible to the changing demands of the management above him. At the same time, he must be responsive to the demands of the work group of which he is a member. He is placed in the difficult position of communicating and implementing new decisions, changed programs and revised production quotas for his work group, although he may have had little part in developing them.

It follows, then, that supervision has a special characteristic: achievement of goals, previously set by management, through the efforts of others. It is in this feature of the supervisor's job that we find the role of a leader in the sense of the following definition: *A leader is that person who most effectively influences group activities toward goal setting and goal achievements.*

This definition is broad. It covers both leaders in groups that come together voluntarily and in those brought together through a work assignment in a factory, store, or government agency. In the natural group, the authority necessary to attain goals is determined by the group membership and is granted by them. In the working group, it is apparent that the establishment of a supervisory position creates a predisposition on the part of employees to accept the authority of the occupant of that position. We cannot, however, assume that mere occupation confers authority sufficient to assure the accomplishment of an organization's goals.

Supervision is different, then, from leadership. The supervisor is expected to fulfill the role of leader but without obtaining a grant of authority from the group he supervises. The supervisor is expected to influence the group in the achieving of goals but is often handicapped by having little influence on the organizational process by which goals are set. The supervisor, because he works in an organizational setting, has the burdens of additional organizational duties and restrictions and requirements arising out of the fact that his position is subordinate to a hierarchy of higher-level supervisors. These differences between leadership and supervision are reflected in our definition: *Supervision is basically a leadership role, in a formal organization, which has as its objective the effective influencing of other employees.*

Even though these differences between supervision and leadership exist, a significant finding of experimenters in this field is that supervisors must be leaders to be successful.

The problem is: How can a supervisor exercise leadership in an organizational setting? We might say that the supervisor is expected to be a natural leader in a situation which does not come about naturally. His situation becomes really difficult in an organization which is more eager to make its supervisors into followers rather than leaders.

LEADERSHIP: NATURAL AND ORGANIZATIONAL

Leadership, in its usual sense of *natural* leadership, and supervision are not the same. In some cases, leadership embraces broader powers and functions than supervision; in other cases, supervision embraces more than leadership. This is true both because of the organization and technical aspects of the supervisor's job and because of the relatively freer setting and inherent authority of the natural leader.

The natural leader usually has much more authority and influence than the supervisor. Group members not only follow his command but prefer it that way. The employee, however, can appeal the supervisor's commands to his union or to the supervisor's superior or to the personnel office. These intercessors represent restrictions on the supervisor's power to lead.

The natural leader can gain greater membership involvement in the group's objectives, and he can change the objectives of the group. The supervisor can attempt to gain employee support only for management's objectives; he cannot set other objectives. In these instances leadership is broader than supervision.

The natural leader must depend upon whatever skills are available when seeking to attain objectives. The supervisor is trained in the administrative skills necessary to achieve management's goals. If he does not possess the requisite skills, however, he can call upon management's technicians.

A natural leader can maintain his leadership, in certain groups, merely by satisfying members' need for group affiliation. The supervisor must maintain his leadership by directing and organizing his group to achieve specific organizational goals set for him and his group by management. He must have a technical competence and a kind of coordinating ability which is not needed by many natural leaders.

A natural leader is responsible only to his group which grants him authority. The supervisor is responsible to management, which employs him, and also to the work group of which he is a member. The supervisor has the exceedingly difficult job of reconciling the demands of two groups frequently in conflict. He is often placed in the untenable position of trying to play two antagonistic roles. In the above instance, supervision is broader than leadership.

ORGANIZATIONAL INFLUENCES ON LEADERSHIP

The supervisor is both a product and a prisoner of the organization wherein we find him. The organization which creates the supervisor's position also obstructs, restricts, and channelizes the exercise of his duties. These influences extend beyond prescribed functional relationships to specific supervisory behavior. For example, even in a face-to-face situation involving one of his subordinates, the supervisor's actions are controlled to a great extent by his organization. His behavior must conform to the organization policy on human relations, rules which dictate personnel procedures, specific prohibitions governing conduct, the attitudes of his own superior, etc. He is not a free agent operating within the limits of his work group. His freedom of action is much more circumscribed than is generally admitted. The organizational influences which limit his leadership actions can be classified as structure, prescriptions, and proscriptions.

The organizational structure places each supervisor's position in context with other designated positions. It determines the relationships between his position and specific positions which impinge on his. The structure of the organization designates a certain position to which he looks for orders and information about his work. It gives a particular status to his position within a pattern of statuses from which he perceives that (1) certain positions are on a par, organizationally, with his, (2) other positions are subordinate, and (3) still others are superior.

The organizational structure determines those positions to which he should look for advice and assistance, and those positions to which he should give advice and assistance.

For instance, the organizational structure has predetermined that the supervisor of a clerical processing unit shall report to a supervisory position in a higher echelon. He shall have certain relationships with the supervisors of the work units which transmit work to and receive work from his unit. He shall discuss changes and clarification of procedures with certain staff units, such as organization and methods, cost accounting, and personnel. He shall consult supervisors of units which provide or receive special work assignments.

The organizational structure, however, establishes patterns other than those of the relationships of positions. These are the patterns of responsibility, authority, and expectations.

The supervisor is responsible for certain activities or results; he is presumably invested with the authority to achieve these. His set of authority and responsibility is interwoven with other sets to the end that all goals and functions of the organization are parceled out in small, manageable lots. This, of course, establishes a series of expectations: a single supervisor can perform his particular set of duties only upon the assumption that preceding or contiguous sets of duties have been, or are being carried out. At the same time, he is aware of the expectations of others that he will fulfill his functional role.

The structure of an organization establishes relationships between specified positions and specific expectations for these positions. The fact that these relationships and expectations are established is one thing; whether or not they are met is another.

PRESCRIPTIONS AND PROSCRIPTIONS

But let us return to the organizational influences which act to restrict the supervisor's exercise of leadership. These are the prescriptions and proscriptions generally in effect in all organizations, and those peculiar to a single organization. In brief these are the *thou shalt's* and the *thou shalt not's*.

Organizations not only prescribe certain duties for individual supervisory positions, they also prescribe specific methods and means of carrying out these duties and maintaining management-employee relations. These include rules, regulations, policy, and tradition. It does no good for the supervisor to say, *This seems to be the best way to handle such-and-such,* if the organization has established a routine for dealing with problems. For good or bad, there are rules that state that firings shall be executed in such a manner, accompanied by a certain notification; that training shall be conducted, and in this manner. Proscriptions are merely negative prescriptions; you may not discriminate against any employee because of politics or race; you shall not suspend any employee without following certain procedures and obtaining certain approvals.

Most of these prohibitions and rules apply to the area of interpersonal relations, precisely the area which is now arousing most interest on the part of administrators and managers. We have become concerned about the contrast between formally prescribed relationships and interpersonal relationships, and this brings us to the often discussed informal organization.

FORMAL AND INFORMAL ORGANIZATIONS

As we well know, the functions and activities of any organization are broken down into individual units of work called positions. Administrators must establish a pattern which will link these positions to each other and relate them to a system of authority and responsibility. Man-to-man are spelled out as plainly as possible for all to understand. Managers, then, build an official structure which we call the formal organization.

In these same organizations, employees react individually and in groups to institutionally determined roles. John, a worker, rides in the same carpool as Joe, a foreman. An unplanned communication develops. Harry, a machinist knows more about high-speed machining than his foreman or anyone else in his shop. An unofficial tool boss comes into being. Mary, who fought with Jane, is promoted over her. Jane now gives Mary's directions. A planned relationship fails to develop. The employees have built a structure which we call the informal organization.

Formal organization is a system of management-prescribed relations between positions in an organization.

Informal organization is a network of unofficial relations between people in an organization.

These definitions might lead us to the absurd conclusion that positions carry out formal activities and that employe4es spend their time in unofficial activities. We must recognize that organizational activities are in all cases carried out by people. The formal structure provides a needed framework within which interpersonal relations occur. What we call informal organization is the complex of normal, natural relations among employees. These personal relationships may be negative or positive. That is, they may impede or aid the achievement of organizational goals. For example, friendship between two supervisors greatly increases the probability of good cooperation and coordination between their sections. On the other hand, *buck passing* nullifies the formal structure by failure to meet a prescribed and expected responsibility.

It is improbable that an ideal organization exists where all activities are carried out in strict conformity to a formally prescribed pattern of functional roles. Informal organization arises because of the incompleteness and ambiguities in the network of formally prescribed relationships, or in response to the needs or inadequacies of supervisors or managers who hold prescribed functional roles in an organization. Many of these relationships are not prescribed by the organizational pattern; many cannot be prescribed; many should not be prescribed.

Management faces the problem of keeping the informal organization in harmony with the mission of the agency. One way to do this is to make sure that all employees have a clear understanding of and are sympathetic with that mission. The issuance of organizational charts, procedural manuals, and functional descriptions of the work to be done by divisions and sections helps communicate management's plans and goals. Issuances alone, of course, cannot do the whole job. They should be accompanied by oral discussion and explanation. Management must ensure that there is mutual understanding and acceptance of charts and procedures. More important is that management acquaint itself with the attitudes, activities, and peculiar brands of logic which govern the informal organization. Only through this type of knowledge can they and supervisors keep informal goals consistent with the agency mission.

SUPERVISION STATUS AND FUNCTIONAL ROLE

A well-established supervisor is respected by the employees who work with him. They defer to his wishes. It is clear that a superior-subordinate relationship has been established. That is, status of the supervisor has been established in relation to other employees of the same work group. This same supervisor gains the respect of employees when he behaves in as certain manner. He will be expected, generally, to follow the customs of the group in such matters as dress, recreation, and manner of speaking. The group has a set of expectations as to his behavior. His position is a functional role which carries with it a collection of rights and obligations.

The position of supervisor usually has a status distinct from the individual who occupies it: it is much like a position description which exists whether or not there is an incumbent. The status of a supervisory position is valued higher than that of an employee position both because of the functional role of leadership which is assigned to it and because of the status symbols of titles, rights, and privileges which go with it.

Social ranking, or status, is not simple because it involves both the position and the man. An individual may be ranked higher than others because of his education, social background, perceived leadership ability, or conformity to group customs and ideals. If such a man is ranked higher by the members of a work group than their supervisor, the supervisor's effectiveness may be seriously undermined.

If the organization does not build and reinforce a supervisor's status, his position can be undermined in a different way. This will happen when managers go around rather than through the supervisor or designate him as a straw boss, acting boss, or otherwise not a real boss.

Let us clarify this last point. A role, and corresponding status, establishes a set of expectations. Employees expect their supervisor to do certain things and to act in certain ways. They are prepared to respond to that expected behavior. When the supervisor's behavior does not conform to their expectations, they are surprised, confused, and ill-at-ease. It becomes necessary for them to resolve their confusion, if they can. They might do this by turning to one of their own members for leadership. If the confusion continues, or their attempted solutions are not satisfactory, they will probably become a poorly motivated, non-cohesive group which cannot function very well.

COMMUNICATION AND THE SUPERVISOR

In a recent survey, railroad workers reported that they rarely look to their supervisor for information about the company. This is startling, at least to us, because we ordinarily think of the supervisor as the link between management and worker. We expect the supervisor to be the prime source of information about the company. Actually, the railroad workers listed the supervisor next to last in the o5rder of their sources of information. Most surprising of all, the supervisors, themselves, stated that rumor and unofficial contacts were their principal sources of information. Here we see one of the reasons why supervisors may not be as effective as management desires.

The supervisor is not only being bypassed by his work group, he is being ignored, and his position weakened, by the very organization which is holding him responsible for the activities of his workers. If he is management's representative to the employee, then management has an obligation to keep him informed of its activities. This is necessary if he is to carry out his functions efficiently and maintain his leadership in the work group. The supervisor is expected to be a source of information; when he is not, his status is not clear, and employees are dissatisfied because he has not lived up to expectations.

By providing information to the supervisor to pass along to employees, we can strengthen his position as leader of the group, and increase satisfaction and cohesion within the group. Because he has more information than the other members, receives information sooner, and passes it along at the proper times, members turn to him as a source and also provide him with information in the hope of receiving some in return. From this, we can see an increase in group cohesiveness because:

- Employees are bound closer to their supervisor because he is *in the know*.
- There is less need to go outside the group for answers
- Employees will more quickly turn to the supervisor for enlightenment

The fact that he has the answers will also enhance the supervisor's standing in the eyes of his men. This increased status will serve to bolster his authority and control of the group and will probably result in improved morale and productivity.

The foregoing, of course, does not mean that all management information should be given out. There are obviously certain policy determinations and discussions which need not or cannot be transmitted to all supervisors. However, the supervisor must be kept as fully informed as possible so that he can answer questions when asked and can allay needless fears and anxieties. Further, the supervisor has the responsibility of encouraging employee questions and submissions of information. He must be able to present information to employees so that it is clearly understood and accepted. His attitude and manner should make it clear that he believes in what he is saying, that the information is necessary or desirable to the group, and that he is prepared to act on the basis of the information.

SUPERVISION AND JOB PERFORMANCE

The productivity of work groups is a product; employees' efforts are multiplied by the supervision they receive. Many investigators have analyzed this relationship and have discovered elements of supervision which differentiate high and low production groups. These researchers have identified certain types of supervisory practices which they classify as *employee-centered* and other types which they classify as *production centered*.

The difference between these two kinds of supervision lies not in specific practices but in the approach or orientation to supervision. The employee-centered supervisor directs most of his efforts toward increasing employee motivation. He is concerned more with realizing the potential energy of persons than with administrative and technological methods of increasing efficiency and productivity. He is the man who finds ways of causing employees to want to work harder with the same tools. These supervisors emphasize the personal relations between their employees and themselves.

Now, obviously, these pictures are overdrawn. No one supervisor has all the virtues of the ideal type of employee-centered supervisor. And, fortunately, no one supervisor has all the bad traits found in many production-centered supervisors. We should remember that the various practices that researchers have fond which distinguish these two kinds of supervision represent the many practices and methods of supervisors of all gradations between these extremes. We should be careful, too, of the implications of the labels attached to the two types. For instance, being production-centered is not necessarily bad, since the principal responsibility of any supervisor is maintaining the production level that is expected of his work group. Being employee-centered may not necessarily be good, if the only result is a happy, chuckling crew of loafers. To return to the researchers' findings, employee-centered supervisors:

- Recommend promotions, transfers, pay increases
- Inform men about what is happening in the company
- Keep men posted on how well they are doing
- Hear complaints and grievances sympathetically
- Speak up for subordinates

Production-centered supervisors, on the other hand, don't do those things. They check on employees more frequently, give more detailed and frequent instructions, don't give reasons for changes, and are more punitive when mistakes are made. Employee-centered supervisors were reported to contribute to high morale and high production, whereas production-centered supervision was associated with lower morale and less production.

More recent findings, however, show that the relationship between supervision and productivity is not this simple. Investigators now report that high production is more frequently associated with supervisory practices which combine employee-centered behavior with concern for production. (This concern is not the same, however, as anxiety about production, which is the hallmark of our production-centered supervisor.) Let us examine these apparently contradictory findings and the premises from which they are derived.

SUPERVISION AND MORALE

Why do supervisory activities cause high or low production? As the name implies, the activities of the employee-centered supervisor tend to relate him more closely and satisfactorily to his workers. The production-centered supervisor's practices tend to separate him from his group and to foster antagonism. An analysis of this difference may answer our question.

Earlier, we pointed out that the supervisor is a type of leader and that leadership is intimately related to the group in which it occurs We discover, now, that an employee-centered supervisor's primary activities are concerned with both his leadership and his group membership. Such a supervisor is a member of a group and occupies a leadership role in that group.

These facts are sometimes obscured when we speak of the supervisor as management's representative, or as the organizational link between management and the employee, or as the end of the chain of command. If we really want to understand what it is we expect of the supervisor, we must remember that he is the designated leader of a group of employees to whom he is bound by interaction and interdependence.

Most of his actions are aimed, consciously or unconsciously, at strengthening membership ties in the group. This includes both making members more conscious that he is a member of their group) and causing members to identify themselves more closely with the group. These ends are accomplished by:

- making the group more attractive to the worker: they find satisfaction of their needs for recognition, friendship, enjoyable work, etc.;
- maintaining open communication: employees can express their views and obtain information about the organization
- giving assistance: members can seek advice on personal problems as well as their work; and
- acting as a buffer between the group and management: he speaks up for his men and explains the reasons for management's decisions.

Such actions both strengthen group cohesiveness and solidarity and affirm the supervisor's leadership position in the group.

DEFINING MORALE

This brings us back to a point mentioned earlier. We had said that employee-centered supervisors contribute to high morale as well as to high production. But how can we explain units which have low morale and high productivity, or vice versa? Usually production and morale are considered separately, partly because they are measured against different criteria and partly because, in some instances, they seem to be independent of each other.

Some of this difficulty may stem from confusion over definitions of morale. Morale has been defined as, or measured by, absences from work, satisfaction with job or company, dissension among members of work groups, productivity, apathy or lack of interest, readiness to help others, and a general aura of happiness as rated by observers. Some of these criteria of morale are not subject to the influence of the supervisor, and some of them are not clearly related to productivity. Definitions like these invite findings of low morale coupled with high production.

Both productivity and morale can be influenced by environmental factors not under the control of group members or supervisors. Such things as plant layout, organizational structure and goals, lighting, ventilation, communications, and management planning may have an adverse or desirable effect.

We might resolve the dilemma by defining morale on the basis of our understanding of the supervisor as leader of a group; morale is the degree of satisfaction of group members with their leadership. In this light, the supervisor's employee-centered activities bear a clear relation to morale. His efforts to increase employee identification with the group and to strengthen his leadership lead to greater satisfaction with that leadership. By increasing group cohesiveness and by demonstrating that his influence and power can aid the group, he is able to enhance his leadership status and afford satisfaction to the group.

SUPERVISION, PRODUCTION, AND MORALE

There are factors within the organization itself which determine whether increased production is possible:

- Are production goals expressed in terms understandable to employees and are they realistic?
- Do supervisors responsible for production respect the agency mission and production goals?
- If employees do not know how to do the job well, does management provide a trainer—often the supervisor—who can teach efficient work methods?

There are other factors within the work group which determine whether increased production will be attained:

- Is leadership present which can bring about the desired level of production?
- Are production goals accepted by employees as reasonable and attainable?
- If group effort is involved, are members able to coordinate their efforts?

Research findings confirm the view that an employee-centered supervisor can achieve higher morale than a production-centered supervisor. Managers may well ask what is the relationship between this and production.

Supervision is production-oriented to the extent that it focuses attention on achieving organizational goals, and plans and devises methods for attaining them; it is employee-centered to the extent that it focuses attention on employee attitudes toward those goals, and plans and works toward maintenance of employee satisfaction.

High productivity and low morale result when a supervisor plans and organizes work efficiently but cannot achieve high membership satisfaction. Low production and high morale result when a supervisor, though keeping members satisfied with his leadership, either has not gained acceptance of organizational goals or does not have the technical competence to achieve them.

The relationship between supervision, morale, and productivity is an interdependent one, with the supervisor playing an integral role due to his ability to influence productivity and morale independently of each other.

A supervisor who can plan his work well has good technical knowledge, and who can install better production methods can raise production without necessarily increasing group satisfaction. On the other hand, a supervisor who can motivate his employees and keep them satisfied with his leadership can gain high production in spite of technical difficulties and environmental obstacles.

CLIMATE AND SUPERVISION

Climate, the intangible environment of an organization made up of attitudes, beliefs, and traditions, plays a large part in morale, productivity, and supervision. Usually when we speak of climate and its relationship to morale and productivity, we talk about the merits of *democratic* versus *authoritarian* climate. Employees seem to produce more and have higher morale in a democratic climate, whereas in an authoritarian climate, the reverse seems to be true or so the researchers tell us. We would do well to determine what these terms mean to supervision.

Perhaps most of our difficulty in understanding and applying these concepts comes from our emotional reactions to the words themselves. For example, authoritarian climate is usually painted as the very blackest kind of dictatorship. This is not surprising, because we are usually expected to believe that it is invariably bad. Conversely, democratic climate is drawn to make the driven snow look impure by comparison.

Now these descriptions are most probably true when we talk about our political processes, or town meetings, or freedom of speech. However, the same labels have been used by social scientists in other contexts and have also been applied to government and business organizations, without it, it seems, any recognition that the meanings and their social values may have changed somewhat

For example, these labels were used in experiments conducted in an informal classroom setting using 11-year-old boys as subjects. The descriptive labels applied to the climate of the setting as well as the type of leadership practiced. When these labels were transferred to a management setting, it seems that many presumed that they principally meant the king of leadership rather than climate. We can see that there is a great difference between the experimental and management settings and that leadership practices for one might be inappropriate for the other.

It is doubtful that formal work organizations can be anything but authoritarian, in that goals are set by management and a hierarchy exists through which decisions and orders from the top are transmitted downward. Organizations are authoritarian by structure and need; direction and control are placed in the hands of a few in order to gain fast and efficient decision making. Now this does not mean to describe a dictatorship. It is merely the recognition of the fact that direction of organizational affairs comes from above. It should be noted that leadership in some natural groups is, in this sense, authoritarian.

Granting that formal organizations have this kind of authoritarian leadership, can there be a democratic climate? Certainly there can be, but we would want to define and delimit this term. A more realistic meaning of democratic climate in organizations is the use of permissive and participatory methods in management-employee relations. That is, a mutual exchange of information and explanation with the granting of individual freedom within certain restricted and defined limits. However, it is not our purpose to debate the merits of authoritarianism versus democracy. We recognize that within the small work group there is a need for freedom from constraint and an increase in participation in order to achieve organizational goals within the framework of the organizational movement.

Another aspect of climate is best expressed by this familiar, and true, saying: actions speak louder than words. Of particular concern to us is this effect of management climate on the behavior of supervisors, particularly in employee-centered activities.

There have been reports of disappointment with efforts to make supervisors ore employee-centered. Managers state that, since research has shown ways of improving human relations, supervisors should begin to practice these methods. Usually a training course in human relations is established; and supervisors are given this training. Managers then sit back and wait for the expected improvements, only to find that there are none.

If we wish to produce changes in the supervisor's behavior, the climate must be made appropriate and rewarding to the changed behavior. This means that top-level attitudes and behavior cannot deny or contradict the change we are attempting to effect. Basic changes in organizational behavior cannot be made with any permanence, unless we provide an environment that is receptive to the changes and rewards those persons who do change.

IMPROVING SUPERVISION

Anyone who has read this far might expect to find *A Dozen Rules for Dealing With Employees* or *29 Steps to Supervisory Success*. We will not provide such a list.

Simple rules suffer from their simplicity. They ignore the complexities of human behavior. Reliance upon rules may cause supervisors to concentrate on superficial aspects of their relations with employees. It may preclude genuine understanding.

The supervisor who relies on a list of rules tends to think of people in mechanistic terms. In a certain situation, he uses *Rule No. 3*. Employees are not treated as thinking and feeling persons, but rather as figures in a formula: Rule 3 applied to employee X = Production.

Employees usually recognize mechanical manipulation and become dissatisfied and resentful. They lose faith in, and respect for, their supervisor, and this may be reflected in lower morale and productivity.

We do not mean that supervisors must become social science experts if they wish to improve. Reports of current research indicate that there are two major parts of their job which can be strengthened through self-improvement: (1) Work planning, including technical skills, and (2) motivation of employees.

The most effective supervisors combine excellence in the administrative and technical aspects of their work with friendly and considerate personal relations with their employees.

CRITICAL PERSONAL RELATIONS

Later in this chapter we shall talk about administrative aspects of supervision, but first let us comment on *friendly and considerate personal relations*. We have discussed this subject throughout the preceding chapters, but we want to review some of the critical supervisory influences on personal relations.

Closeness of Supervision: The closeness of supervision has an important effect on productivity and morale. Mann and Dent found that supervisors of low-producing units supervise very closely, while high-producing supervisors exercise only general supervision. It was found that the low-producing supervisors:

- check on employees more frequently
- give more detailed and frequent instructions
- limit employee's freedom to do job in own way

Workers who felt less closely supervised reported that they were better satisfied with their jobs and the company. We should note that the manner or attitude of the supervisor has an important bearing on whether employees perceive supervision as being close or general.

These findings are another way of saying that supervision does not mean standing over the employee and telling him what to do and when and how to do it. The more effective supervisor tells his employees what is required, giving general instructions.

COMMUNICATION

Supervisors of high-production units consider communication as one of the most important aspects of their job. Effective communication is used by these supervisors to achieve better interpersonal relations and improved employee motivation. Low-production supervisors do not rate communications as highly important.

High-producing supervisors find that an important aid to more effective communication is listening. They are ready to listen to both personal problems or interests and questions about the work. This does not mean that they are *nosey* or meddle in their employees' personal lives, but rather that they show a willingness to listen, and do listen, if their employees wish to discuss problems.

These supervisors inform employees about forthcoming changes in work; they discuss agency policy with employees; and they make sure that each employee knows how well he is doing. What these supervisors do is use two-way communication effectively. Unless the supervisor freely imparts information, he will not receive information in return.

Attitudes and perception are frequently affected by communication or the lack of it. Research surveys reveal that many supervisors are not aware of their employees' attitudes, nor do they know what personal reactions their supervision arouses. Through frank discussion with employees, they have been surprised to discover employee beliefs about which they were ignorant. Discussion sometimes reveals that the supervisor and his employees have totally different impressions about the same event. The supervisor should be constantly on the alert for misconceptions about his words and deeds. He must remember that, although his actions are perfectly clear to himself, they may be, and frequently are, viewed differently by employees.

Failure to communicate information results in misconceptions and false assumptions. What you say and how you say it will strongly affect your employees' attitudes and perceptions. By giving them available information, you can prevent misconceptions; by discussion, you may be able to change attitudes; by questioning, you can discover what the perceptions and assumptions really are. And it need hardly be added that actions should conform very closely to words.

If we were to attempt to reduce the above discussion on communication to rules, we would have a long list which would be based on one cardinal principle: Don't make assumptions!

- Don't assume that your employees know; tell them.
- Don't assume that you know how they feel; find out.
- Don't assume that they understand; clarify.

20 SUPERVISORY HINTS

1. Avoid inconsistency.
2. Always give employees a chance to explain their action before taking disciplinary action. Don't allow too much time for a "cooling off" period before disciplining an employee.
3. Be specific in your criticisms.
4. Delegate responsibility wisely.
5. Do not argue or lose your temper, and avoid being impatient.
6. Promote mutual respect and be fair, impartial, and open-minded.
7. Keep in mind that asking for employees' advice and input can be helpful in decision making.
8. If you make promises, keep them.
9. Always keep the feelings, abilities, dignity and motives of your staff in mind.
10. Remain loyal to your employees' interests.
11. Never criticize employees in front of others, or treat employees like children.
12. Admit mistakes. Don't place blame on your employees, or make excuses.
13. Be reasonable in your expectations, give complete instructions, and establish well-planned goals.
14. Be knowledgeable about office details and procedures, but avoid becoming bogged down in details.
15. Avoid supervising too closely or too loosely. Employees should also view you as an approachable supervisor.
16. Remember that employees' personal problems may affect job performance, but become involved only when appropriate.
17. Work to develop workers, and to instill a feeling of cooperation while working toward mutual goals.
18. Do not overpraise or underpraise, be properly appreciative.
19. Never ask an employee to discipline someone for you.
20. A complaint, even if unjustified, should be taken seriously.

NOTES

www.ingramcontent.com/pod-product-compliance
Lightning Source LLC
Chambersburg PA
CBHW081828300426
44116CB00014B/2517